NEW REFORM
RESPONSA

ALUMNI SERIES OF THE HEBREW UNION COLLEGE PRESS

NEW REFORM
RESPONSA

by

SOLOMON B. FREEHOF, D.D.

Rabbi Emeritus, Rodef Shalom Temple, Pittsburgh

THE HEBREW UNION COLLEGE PRESS

1980

Library of Congress Cataloging in Publication Data

Freehof, Solomon Bennett, 1892-
  New Reform responsa.

  (Alumni series of the Hebrew Union College Press
ISSN 0192-2904)
  Includes index.
  1. Responsa—1800-   2. Reform Judaism—
Ceremonies and practices. I. Title.
BM522.36.R376   296.1'8   80-18218
ISBN 0-87820-110-6

Manufactured in the United States of America

This book is published under the auspices of the Rabbinic Alumni Association of Hebrew Union College–Jewish Institute of Religion. A quinquennial fund to which its members contribute is set aside for the specific purpose of encouraging members of the Association to pursue studies in Judaism with the prospect of publication. We gratefully acknowledge the contribution made by the Rodef Shalom Congregation, Pittsburgh, Pennsylvania, toward the publication of this volume.

ALFRED GOTTSCHALK, *President*
Hebrew Union College—
    Jewish Institute of Religion

NORMAN KAHAN, *President*
Rabbinic Alumni Association

WALTER JACOB, *Chairman*
Publications Committee of the
    Rabbinic Alumni Association

To the blessed memory of my dear brother
LOUIS J. FREEHOF
His life was selfless service.

CONTENTS

Introduction   1
1   Naming the Sanctuary After an Individual   7
2   An Operetta in the Sanctuary   11
3   Printed *Mezuzahs*   17
4   *Tallis* at Torah Reading   20
5   The Disused Ark   24
6   Dispute over Candle-Lighting and *Kiddush*   28
7   Gentiles' Part in the Sabbath Service   33
8   Cemetery Work on Rosh Hashonah   37
9   Titles in Memorial List   41
10 *Succah* and Artificial Fruit   46
11 *Lulav* and *Esrog* after Succos   48
12 A Glass *Mezuzah*   53
13 The Signs of the Zodiac on Synagogue Windows   56
14 Circumcising the Child of an Unmarried Couple   58
15 Kidney Transplants   62
16 The Hospice   67
17 Questions Concerning Proselytes   72
18 An Incomplete Conversion   75
19 Ownership of the Body of the Dead   79
20 A Former Christian Cemetery   85
21 Gentiles Buried in a Jewish Cemetery   88
22 Aged Parent to Nursing Home   92
23 An Unfilled Grave   97
24 Freezing a Body for Later Funeral   100
25 Burial in a National Cemetery   105
26 Congregation Using Cemetery Money   109
27 Not Using the *Chevra Kadisha*   114
28 Quicklime on the Body   117
29 Post-Funeral Eulogy   119
30 *Shiva* in Jerusalem   125
31 Comforting the Bereaved on the Sabbath   130

32   Visiting the Bereaved   133
33   Mourning for the Cremated   139
34   Body Lost But Found Later   142
35   Is a Tombstone Mandatory?   147
36   Covering the Casket   152
37   The Undertaking Business   158
38   The Competing Gentile Undertaker   164
39   Rebates from a Building Fund   168
40   Temple Membership and Charity   175
41   A Survivor's Sense of Guilt   179
42   Wedding Before the Open Ark   182
43   Apostate Wedding Attendants   189
44   Remarriage of Russian Immigrants   193
45   Remarriage of a Widower   198
46   Insemination with Mixed Seed   202
47   The Test-tube Baby   205
48   The Transplanted Ovum   213
49   Assembling a School Prayerbook   219
50   Malpractice Suits and the Physician   224
51   Deprogramming Young People   231
52   All-Adult Apartments   236
53   The "Unwanted" Child   239
Inquiries:
 1   Halachah and Space Travel   243
 2   Salt for the Bread Blessing   247
 3   Hypnotism   250
 4   Reform and Spiritualism   252
 5   Reform and *Mamzerus*   256
 6   Funeral Folklore: Keys in the Coffin   262
 7   *Charoses*   265
 8   Distribution of Laws in Jewish Legal Literature   267

INTRODUCTION

Rashi, commenting on the first verse of Malachi, cites the *Mechilta* to the effect that all the Prophets stood on Mount Sinai and there were given their prophecy. This is an expression of the frequently voiced idea that Judaism has always been the same, from Sinai to this day, and is a natural point of pride in an historic religion. The Roman Catholic Church likewise considers that its doctrine and its practice are *semper et ubique,* forever and everywhere the same.

As far as Judaism is concerned, this eternal changelessness should not really be its greatest pride. The very opposite is much more admirable and remarkable, namely, the adaptability of Judaism to drastic change. For centuries Judaism was a priest-dominated religion. The people were only spectators as the ritual was carried out by the sons of Aaron. Then there was a complete change. Since the destruction of the Temple, priests were in effect deposed. They have only a residual function, and the whole religion is maintained and carried out by laymen. Judaism was once an agricultural religion. Its festivals and a large number of its observances depended upon the agriculture of the land of Israel. Then it became a completely urban religion, completely divorced from the soil. Judaism was once, for many centuries, the religion of a compact people, and it became a religion of scattered fragments which managed to maintain its sense of unity over seas and continents. All these vast changes were lived through. It is

1

doubtful whether any historic religion exists that has gone through such tremendous changes and adjusted to them all.

These changes are a matter of history and are known to all. But there is another change taking place today to which we hope Judaism will once more be able to adjust. This change is to a large extent subsurface and is only partially realized and acknowledged. It is the revolution in Jewish practice which affects all branches of the faith in almost every country in the world, but especially in the western world.

It would be extremely difficult to obtain trustworthy statistics as to how many of the historic Jewish observances are being neglected and in which groups in the Jewish world society which rituals are neglected most. One need only consider the complicated rules of feminine hygiene. Questions on this matter filled the responsa of earlier centuries. If one would inquire in any western city how many Jewish women in a large Jewish community use the *mikvah* regularly, one would have an idea of how this large section of Jewish religious practice has fallen away.

Two or three generations ago, all Jewish business disputes were settled in rabbinical courts. How many of such disputes are still settled without the use of the civil courts? Jacob Ettlinger, in Hamburg a century ago, had to decide whether a Jew who violated the Sabbath could be called up to the Torah. It was a new question then. But today, how many Jewish businessmen feel that they can no longer maintain strict observance of the Sabbath? To what extent are all the detailed laws of meat and milk dishes still carefully observed? Clearly, there is a vast neglect of Jewish religious observance all through the western world.

While it would be difficult through questionnaires to obtain a clear picture of this vast change in Jewish life, some indication of it may be observed by making a statistical comparison of the contents of modern books of responsa and those of earlier generations. Whole sections of Jewish law that filled the responsa books of a hundred and two hundred years ago are no longer dealt with in present-day responsa books. If a modern respondent will have, let us say, fifty questions in the business laws of *Choshen Mishpot,* most of them will be just textual disputes between rabbis, and rarely will there be any actual cases.

This vast change in observance is well understood, although not openly discussed by modernist movements in Judaism such as Conservatism and Reform Judaism. Conservatism, on the basis of a fine store of Halachic learning, believes that the Halachah is in its nature so flexible that it can adjust itself to the modern situation. And, indeed, the movement has made gallant and learned efforts, especially in the field of divorce. Yet no writer in the movement has openly acknowledged the vast extent of nonobservance of traditional Jewish law among its section of modern Jews.

In this regard Reform is more open. It not only is aware of the widespread neglect of traditional observance, but in certain important cases it has consciously adjusted itself. It is a fact, for example, that tens of thousands (we will never know how many) Jewish women, divorced in the civil courts, have remarried without receiving a *get* from the ex-husband. This fact is a reality in almost every stratum of Jewish life. Yet Reform has made an open declaration about it, accepting the full validity of civil divorce, thus freeing the Jewish woman from dependence upon the consent of her ex-husband before she can remarry. So it has been with the general Reform emphasis on the spiritual and ethical teachings of Judaism and the resultant deprecation of the ceremonial observances, which in many instances had fallen away anyhow. The attitude of Reform amounts to the closest approach of any section of Judaism to the real revolution taking place in Jewish observance.

That being the case, it seems strange that in Reform Judaism there is a revival of interest in the Halachic literature. The Central Conference of American Rabbis has had a Responsa Committee and published responsa from the very beginning. In the last two decades at least six hundred Reform responsa have been published. One would imagine that Reform, with its emphasis on the spiritual and ethical rather than the ceremonial and ritual, would be the last of the modern religious movements to work so assiduously in the field of the Halachah.

It is not easy to answer just why this has happened. There are many partial reasons. One is a growing awareness in the movement that the Halachic literature is the most continuous expression of Jewish religious thought all these many centuries. To be part of that literature is perhaps the most genuine contact with the one form of Jewish religious self-expression which has remained unbroken through the centuries. But what can the movement seek and hope to find in this legal literature, which defines so carefully every detail of all the commandments and, in the case of the code of Maimonides, even the details of the sacrificial cult which will be reinstituted when the Temple

will be rebuilt with the coming of the Messiah? At a time
when so many observances in Jewish life are falling away,
the interest of Reform in Halachah is not a reversion to
Orthodoxy but a return to unity with Jewish history.
Reform is not seeking more commandments to re-adopt. It
is seeking guidance for the observances which its people
now maintain. The Halachic literature is dominated by the
total spirit of Judaism. The Prophets live in the Halachah
as well as in the Haftorah; so for those observances which
live among us, we seek the guidance, not of the details in
the Halachah, but what Montesquieu called "the spirit of
the law" and the rabbis before him called *ruach
chachamim.*

As far as Reform Judaism is concerned, it is not too
difficult to find out which are the active observances. It
seems that the questions asked most often are those dealing
with family life, marriage, Bar Mitzvah and Bas Mitzvah,
and death and burial; also questions about congregational
life and its organization. In these matters, which are the
living observances, Reform seeks help from the great
religious continuum, the Halachic literature, and so Reform responsa are continually written.

NAMING THE SANCTUARY AFTER AN INDIVIDUAL

QUESTION:

The congregation has been searching for major memorial gifts. One suggestion has recently been made to name the sanctuary itself after a departed member. Should this be done? (Asked by Rabbi Murray Blackman, New Orleans, Louisiana.)

ANSWER:

THERE ARE a number of precedents in the Jewish past for naming a synagogue after an individual, so that thereafter it would always be referred to by his name. In Egypt, in the Greek period, there was a synagogue dedicated to King Ptolemy and Queen Berenice. Philo refers to synagogues in Rome named for the Roman emperors. There was an "Augustus Synagogue" and a "Tiberius Synagogue." Of course, these particular namings of synagogues in Alexandria and Rome were for the necessary political purpose of securing and protecting the Jewish community by honoring the emperor and thus soliciting his protection.

But a less political reason and a more spiritual one is indicated in the occasional naming of synagogues after Biblical personalities. Thus the Talmud (*Eruvin* 21a) speaks of a synagogue named in honor of Daniel *(Kenishta d' Daniel)*. In Aleppo there were three synagogues named after Moses. And also in the Near East there were some synagogues named after Ezra. Also, there were synagogues named for Elijah the Prophet. This practice finds some echo in modern Jewry. We have temples called Isaiah, and such. But these were names of the Bible personalities, not names which have been perpetuated because of a donation to the congregation.

Yet there are actually some cases where synagogues *were* named for donors. But strangely enough, as far as I can discover, this practice was limited to one historic city, namely, to the ancient Jewish community of Prague. In Prague there were at least four synagogues named after donors. One of them was the "Meisel Synagogue," named after the well-known sixteenth-century leader of the Prague Jewish community, Mordecai Meisel. This name of the synagogue persists to this day after four centuries, although I believe the Communists have converted the Meisel Synagogue into a museum. Also in Prague there was a "Pinkes Synagogue," named for Phineas Horowitz, built and rebuilt by that rabbi's descendants; a synagogue named the "Popper Synagogue" after a donor; and in memory of the donor, Salkind Zigeuner, there was a "Zigeuner Synagogue."

Other than this custom in Prague, I do not know of any other synagogue in any well-known Jewish community named for a donor. This is rather surprising, for Prague was a very great community with famous rabbis, and one might have expected that its example would spread to other Jewish communities. There may be other synagogues so named, but I do not know of any. Evidently, then, if the example of Prague does not seem to have been widely followed, there must be some objections, voiced or unvoiced, to the idea.

Possibly the objection is a purely practical one, and what this objection might be can be understood by examples from the secular world. Andrew Carnegie was one of the first great philanthropists in America. The libraries and the cultural institute he established in Pittsburgh all bear his name. But now the money of the Carnegie Foundation seems less available, while the needs of these institutions have become great. They are appealing to the general public for help, but they are experiencing serious difficulty in receiving donations because people feel that if the institution bears Carnegie's name, let his family support it. Even with smaller gifts, there is sometimes a danger in identifying the gifts with a specific name. In our own congregation, the main temple organ was named after a generous donor of three generations ago. The family no longer is available for donations, and the organ requires rehabilitation at considerable cost. Now the congregation finds it especially difficult to obtain the necessary gifts from donors because the potential donors feel that since the organ is named for this one family, the family should continue to maintain it. This situation is likely to become especially serious with regard to the sanctuary itself. As the years go by, there is an increasing need for funds for upkeep or reconstruction of the sanctuary, and the very fact that the sanctuary is named for one person, while it may indeed be of great help for the present, nevertheless in the long run will become a serious detriment. Of course, a large stained-glass window or even a smaller chapel, neither of which is likely to need constant donations for upkeep, can perhaps be safely named for an individual donor, but not the temple itself, which will always need additional funds for upkeep. All this is, of course, a practical reason. It might be mentioned that in New York the Free Synagogue has been renamed "The Stephen Wise Free Synagogue," but this was done to honor the founding rabbi of the synagogue and is not likely to evoke later financial repercussions.

But there is also a relevant principle in Jewish traditional law which must be borne in mind, namely, that if the congregation does decide to name the sanctuary after a donor, and if this decision proves later to have been a mistake, then it is against Jewish traditional law to reverse that action and to restore the original name (such as Sinai or Sholom) to the sanctuary. This law is stated in the Talmud in *Arachin* 6b, in Maimonides, *Matnas Aniim* 8:6, and in the *Shulchan Aruch, Yore Deah* 259:3. The law states that when a gift has been made to the congregation, then as long as the name appended to the gift is still remembered, no changes may be made (see also *Modern Reform Responsa,* pp. 141 ff.).

This, then, is the situation. While some ancient synagogues, for political reasons, were named after Roman emperors, and while particularly in the city of Prague there were indeed four synagogues named for donors, the custom never spread to the rest of Jewry, evidently because of the practical reasons mentioned above and also because of the traditional law that as long as the name is still remembered, the action may not be rescinded.

2

AN OPERETTA IN THE SANCTUARY

QUESTION:

Our congregation gave a presentation of the opera *The Mikado,* in the synagogue sanctuary. The receipts were of great help to the congregation, which was in financial straits. The presentation also created a favorable impression in the general community. However, certain members raised an objection, feeling that it is improper to have secular music of this kind in the sanctuary. Also, a second question was raised as follows: If we had another operetta in the social hall (which is, in effect, an elongation of the end of the sanctuary opposite the Ark), the people then would be sitting with their backs to the Ark. Would this be permissible? (Asked by Rabbi Sheldon Ezring, New Milford, Connecticut.)

ANSWER:

THE QUESTION of the propriety of music, especially instrumental music, has received considerable discussion in the Halachah. Joseph Caro, in the *Shulchan Aruch* (*Orach Chayim* 560:3), as a mark of mourning for the destruction of the Temple, forbids the listening to instrumental music anywhere. But Isserles says that people are now lenient on this matter and permit the listening and the use of instrumental music for the purposes of *mitzvah,* such as marriages, etc. Modern music and instrumental music in relation (more specifically) to the synagogue and its service was discussed in a famous essay of Judah Leon of Modena, Rabbi of Venice (see the responsum and the discussion in my *Treasury of Responsa,* pp. 160 ff.). He considers that the knowledge of music would lead to enhancement of the mood of worship and therefore should be encouraged.

In modern times, a negative and puritanical objection to music (which would, of course, apply to an operetta) was given under rather tragic circumstances by Yechiel Weinburg of the Orthodox seminary in Berlin. It was in the earlier Nazi times, when Jews were prohibited from attending symphony concerts. The liberal or Reform synagogue, therefore, gave symphony concerts in its sanctuary, and the Jewish music-lovers of Berlin, including many Orthodox, attended. Weinberg was asked whether the Orthodox synagogue might not give such concerts in its sanctuary so that the people would not stray from Orthodoxy. In general he forbids it, but he adds that if it must be, then at least a psalm should be recited to give the music a religious mood (cf. *Current Reform Responsa,* pp. 33 ff.).

But, of course, all this objection to music in general, and especially to music in the synagogue, represents a puritanical attitude and a gloom of grief which can hardly apply to the mood of a modern congregation. See the whole discussion in *Current Reform Responsa.* So, in general, one may say, considering that there *are* some Orthodox leniencies as to music, that certainly a liberal congregation should have no objection to music in the sanctuary.

However, since some members felt that an operetta (or

this operetta) was inappropriate in the sanctuary itself, let us consider the question from this point of view. Let us assume the extreme position that Jews ought not to listen to such an operetta altogether (as Caro would say), and then certainly it should not be presented in the sanctuary. As to this specific question, there is a long and detailed discussion by the premier Orthodox authority in America, Moses Feinstein, in his *Igros Moshe (Orach Chayim #*31). The specific question with which he deals in this responsum is the practice (followed in a large metropolis like New York) for various halls and possibly night clubs to be rented for special High Holiday services. As to this, his specific question is: May a place which is used for unseemly purposes be used for Jewish worship? He bases his opinion on the fact that the Talmud prefers that one pray in the same place where he studies *(Berachos* 8a, *Orach Chayim* 90:18). Since studying the Torah is perhaps the highest of all virtues, this indicates that the moral atmosphere associated with a place helps the effectiveness of the prayers recited there, and therefore Moses Feinstein concludes that the contrary is also true—that a place where unworthy activity takes place would be harmful to the effectiveness of worship. But he also considers a contrary fact, namely, that God's presence is always near where a *minyan* of people worship regularly *(Berachos* 8a). Therefore, one may say that in general he decides that a nightclub or some such place would have a negative effect upon worship held there. However, a place where a *minyan* of worshipers regularly utter their prayers *always* has the blessing of the presence of the *Shechinah*. The presence of the *Shechinah* where people regularly worship as a synagogue is unaffected even if something unworthy has occurred there. He cites the *Be'er Hetev* to *Orach Chayim* 151:1, that even if some ugly sin were committed in the synagogue, it does not affect the suitability of the place for prayer. And, in fact, the *Magen Avraham* to *Orach Chayim* 154 cites an even more drastic evil that may occur in the synagogue. If, for example, idols were brought in there (and then, of course, removed), the worthiness of the synagogue for prayer would not be impaired thereby (see *Magen Avraham* to *Orach Chayim* 154:17). Both citations are originally from the responsa of Elijah Mizrachi.

Thus Moses Feinstein makes a distinction between a place which is regularly used for unworthy purposes and a synagogue in which occasionally some unworthy act has occurred. The synagogue retains its sanctity. Therefore we may conclude that even if having given the operetta was an act unworthy of the synagogue, as some members seem to think, the suitability of the synagogue for worship is not impaired thereby. Incidentally, with regard to the hall hired for High Holiday worship, he says, it is unworthy as long as it is merely hired, but if it is bought outright and transformed into a synagogue where a regular *minyan* worships, its past would not affect its present sanctity.

All this discussion assumes (for the sake of argument) the extreme puritanical position that the operetta as such somehow was wrong and evil. Actually, this is not so. Gilbert and Sullivan's operetta is charming and delightful, and there is nothing immoral in it. Besides, the fact that it aided in the maintenance of the synagogue and created good will in the community is certainly a justification for it and similarly decent operettas to be given there. Of course, it might be advisable for a rather extensive and opaque partition to be put up before the Ark.

Now as to the second question. In case future operettas were given in the social hall, where the seats would have the audience sitting with their backs to the Ark (at some distance away), is there any objection to that? First, this is a separate enclosure, and therefore, there is no objection to the direction in which people sit there. But let us say that the audience flows over from the back of the social hall into the sanctuary and there, facing the stage of the social hall, they will sit with their backs to the Ark (at some distance away). Is there any objection in Jewish tradition to this?

It is the custom in our Ashkenazic synagogues for the congregation to sit facing the Ark, but in Sephardic synagogues there are almost no seats facing the Ark. They are all sideways, along the north and south walls. But even with us, the tradition is that the elders sit facing the congregation, and as the *Shulchan Aruch* and especially the *Tur* clearly say, they sit facing the congregation and their back is to the Ark (see *Tur, Orach Chayim* 150, end, and *Shulchan Aruch, Orach Chayim* 150:4). Also, when we take a Torah from the Ark, we (for a brief time) turn our back to the Ark. When the *maggid* preaches, he has his back to the Ark all through his sermon. Of course, the leaders and the congregation, at the appropriate places in the service, turn to face the Ark; but as indicated, during the rest of the time, the leaders sit with their backs to the Ark. There is no objection to this.

To sum up: Some puritanical residue of mourning for the destruction of the Temple tends to discourage and even prohibit listening to any instrumental music. But as Isserles and especially Modena indicate, music, vocal and instrumental, is increasingly permissible, certainly so in liberal congregations. Furthermore, even if an operetta like *The Mikado* were evil in mood, it would not affect the sanctity of the synagogue. Actually *The Mikado* is a decent operetta, and its production has helped maintain the synagogue, which is of course a *mitzvah*. As for people sitting with their backs to the Ark at the far end of the synagogue, this is not objected to anywhere in the law. It is clear that the congregation may continue without objection to give such operettas. Yet it would be advisable, because of the objections of some of the members, to have the Ark shielded by a complete partition.

3

PRINTED MEZUZAHS

QUESTION:

A gift shop in the congregation had sold a number of *mezuzahs* to members and others. Then it was discovered that the *mezuzahs* were printed instead of written by hand as the Halachah requires. What shall the congregation do? There is some doubt on the matter because a public admission of this deception might create scorn for Judaism in general. (Asked by Rabbi Jack Segal, Houston, Texas.)

ANSWER:

THE QUESTION is a serious one and also delicate. There have been in the last few years a number of widely publicized false and deceptive schemes in which rabbis and Jewish organizations, such as *yeshivos,* have been involved. The publicity given to these unfortunate occurrences has undoubtedly, in some circles, caused a certain amount of scorn and contempt for organized Jewish religious life. Therefore, especially these days, the congregation is justly hesitant about creating further *chillul ha-shem,* a profanation of the Name of God and the good name of the congregation. How, then should the congregation act in this delicate situation?

First of all, it must be realized that what has occurred—the selling of printed instead of written *mezuzahs,* i.e., *posul mezuzahs*—is a sin. The nature of

17

the sin is a violation of the commandment, "Thou shalt not put a stumbling-block before the blind" *(lifney iver),* that is to say, the sin of leading unsuspecting people to commit a sin. To put up these illegal *mezuzahs* on their doorposts certainly leads people to neglect putting up kosher *mezuzahs,* as they are commanded to do, and therefore causes them to sin by violating the positive commandment of affixing a *mezuzah.* Unfortunately, this sin of "causing the blind to stumble" *(lifney iver)* is not unusual in America; in fact it is widely practiced. J. D. Eisenstein, in his *Ozar Dinim,* p. 215a, makes a public record of those who print *mezuzahs* and sell them, and he states correctly that they are committing the sin of "putting a stumbling-block," etc.

Whose sin is it in the situation spoken about in the question? Definitely it is *not* the sin of the congregation, unless, of course, those in charge of the gift shop knew that the *mezuzahs* were printed but concealed the fact. This is certainly not the situation. They bought the *mezuzahs* as kosher *mezuzahs* and sold them as such. If it is a sin on their part, it is an unintentional one and, therefore, forgivable. The real sinners are the manufacturers and the wholesalers who sold them to the gift shop. This being the case, the congregation has nothing of which to be ashamed.

Nevertheless, it cannot keep silent (as it might prefer to do), for to do so would be a conscious sin on its part of *lifney iver.* To know, as the congregation knows well, that the *mezuzahs* are *posul,* and nevertheless to let the people affix them, would certainly be a sinful act of conscious deception which the congregation cannot possibly permit itself.

Clearly, what the congregation must do is this: It must frankly inform the members that it has now bought a large number of kosher *mezuzahs* and is ready, without charge, to exchange them for the non-kosher *mezuzahs* which it had inadvertently sold. As for the non-kosher ones, those who wish to keep them may use them as pendants, as some do, but they cannot be used in fulfillment of the commandment of *mezuzah*. In other words, the congregation has a duty to prevent the members from committing the sin of neglecting the positive commandment of putting up a *mezuzah*, and it must frankly make up for its unintended mistake. If this procedure is followed, no blame will be felt against the congregation. Nevertheless, we must all bear the shame of the fact that there are certain manufacturers who are willing to mislead the Jewish people. In fact, we must do more than be ashamed of it. Public protest against them should be made through the appropriate national organizations.

4

TALLIS AT TORAH READING

QUESTION:

The congregation has introduced a rule that those who are called up to the Torah at the Friday night Torah reading must wear a *tallis*. A number of members object to the wearing of the *tallis* when called to the Torah. Does the congregation have the right to establish this rule, and if it does, has the member the right to object to it? (Asked by Isidore Kornzweig, Santa Barbara, California.)

ANSWER:

IT IS NOT clear from the question what was the basis of the member's objection. Did he object because he feels that as a Reform Jew he does not believe in these ceremonials, or did he object as a traditional Jew because the *tallis* is not to be worn at night? This indefiniteness goes further: It is not clear on the basis of Jewish law whether the congregation has the right to make this regulation, nor is it clear whether a member has the right to object, once the regulation has been made.

First, as to the right of the congregation in this matter: Of course, as has already been noted in the letter of inquiry, it is contrary to traditional practice to have the Torah reading on Friday night. The Torah is read in the morning on Sabbaths and holidays and Mondays and Thursdays, and also in the afternoon on Saturdays. Reform

introduced the Friday evening Torah reading because
Friday evening was the best-attended service. (By the
way, the late Friday evening service, i.e., after dark, is
itself a reform; traditionally the service should be at
sunset.) However, this new custom of Friday evening
Torah reading has by now become established in Reform
and is not entirely unjustified even from the legal point of
view (see the discussion in *Modern Reform Responsa,* pp.
14 ff.).

But now, to this (by-now-established) custom of reading the Torah on Friday night, this congregation proposes
an additional change to require the *tallis* to be worn by
those who are called up to the Torah. This, too, is against
the established custom. The *tallis* is not to be worn at night
(see the rule given in *Orach Chayim* 18:1 that night is not
the time for the fringed garment). Of course the cantor
wears the *tallis* more often than the people. He wears it
whenever he officiates, but the people wear the *tallis* only
in the morning and also for *Musaf.* Also, the people wear
the *tallis* on Yom Kippur night, but even so, according to
the rule, the *tallis* must be put on and the blessing recited
before dark.

Therefore the question arises whether a congregation
may add another observance which, too, is contrary to an
established custom. Perhaps the justification is that the
congregation considers that the wearing of the *tallis* at the
Torah reading adds to the dignity of the service, and that
motive is considered by the law as an important one. Much
is allowed for the sake of *kovode ha-tzibbur.*

Now the other half of the problem is this: Has the
member the right to object to being compelled to wear a

tallis if called up to the Torah? I think it is clear that he would have had the right to object to the adoption of the custom when it was debated at the temple meeting, but can he object once the ruling has been adopted? The answer to that question depends on whether a member has the *right* to be called up to the Torah. Is being called up to the Torah a right that a member can demand or is it, perhaps, a *mitzvah* that he must fulfill, or is it just a privilege which the congregation confers upon a member? All these matters are discussed fully in *Current Reform Responsa,* pp. 62 ff. (a responsum which also appeared in the *CCAR Yearbook,* Vol. 72).

Naturally, if it is only a privilege conferred upon a member to be called to the Torah, then the congregation has the right to deny the privilege if it feels that the man coming to the Torah without the *tallis* impairs the dignity of the service. The Talmud has a strong precedent for the denial of the right to come up to the Torah, in order by this denial to maintain the *kovode ha-tzibbur,* the dignity of the congregation. The Talmud in *Megillah* 23a says that a woman has the right to be called up to the Torah on the Sabbath, but we do not do it because of the "dignity of the congregation." This is given as a law in *Orach Chayim* 282:3.

If, therefore, the calling to the Torah is only a privilege, then the congregation has the right to withhold this privilege for the sake of the dignity of the service. But suppose it *is* a duty or a right, then the congregation would not have the prerogative of denying the man his rights. (In the responsum mentioned, a case is cited of a Yemenite Jew in Israel who actually sued the congregation for his "right" to be called to the Torah, which had been denied him.) One might say that to a certain limited extent it is a right and a duty to be called to the Torah, but only with regard to the following limits: A Kohen by tradition has the right to be called first to the Torah and a Levite second. If they are the only Kohen or Levite in the *shul* on the Sabbath, they have the right to demand to be called up. This right, of course, would not apply in a Reform congregation, since Reform has abolished the distinction between Kohen, Levite, and Israelite. But there still remain the following rights: a man to be called up on *Yahrzeit*; a prospective bridegroom to be called up before his marriage; and a father at the naming of a child or at a son's Bar Mitzvah.

These established rights give us a way out of the dilemmas caused by the fact that in general the rights of the congregation in this matter and the right of the member are not absolutely definite in the law. The decision arrived at perhaps should be as follows: If a member has, for example, a child Bar Mitzvah, at which time he has the right and the duty to come up to the Torah, he should be permitted under these circumstances to come, whether he wears a *tallis* or not, since the congregation has no right to prevent him from fulfilling a religious duty. But under all other and ordinary circumstances, the congregation, for the dignity of the service *(kovode ha-tzibbur)*, has the right to insist on the observance of its rules in this matter.

5

THE DISUSED ARK

QUESTION:

The congregation has an Ark which is no longer in use. A proposal has been made to convert the Ark into a bookcase to be used in the instruction of retarded children. Is such a use of a disused Ark permissible? (Asked by Rabbi Richard A. Zionts, Shreveport, Louisiana.)

ANSWER:

THE QUESTION of the proper disposal of unused or unusable sacred objects has received detailed discussion in the law from the time of the Mishnah down to our day. What disposal or use may be made of unusable sacred objects like worn-out Torah covers or the Torah itself or the Ark in which it is contained, etc.? The answer to this depends on the rank of the particular object in the order of sanctity. There are a number of classifications used for sacred objects. The most sacred object of all is the Sefer Torah. The objects that are appurtenances to the Sefer Torah, such as the covers, the bands, and the Ark in which it is kept, are all called *tashmishey kedusha* (accessories to the sacred). Then there is a second class of objects of lower sanctity which involves, not the Torah, which is the most sacred, but the *shofar,* the *tefillin,* the *tallis,* etc. The appurtenances of these objects—such as, for example, the sack in

24

which *tefillin* are kept—are called *tashmishey mitzvah* (accessories to the commandments). The rule covering the two classes is definite enough. The appurtenances of the sacred, i.e., of the Torah, if no longer usable, must be hidden away or buried. But the appurtenances of *mitzvah,* like the sack for the *tefillin* when no longer used, may be thrown away (*Megillah* 26b).

Within the more sacred class, the *tashmishey kedusha* (i.e., objects involved with the Sefer Torah), there is a gradation of sanctity. This is first mentioned in the Mishnah at the beginning of Chapter 3 of *Megillah* and is developed in the Talmud (ad loc.) The rule there given can be summed up as follows: One may dispose of these sacred things provided that with the money derived, something more sacred may be purchased. Thus the community may sell the public square (where only occasional fast-day services are held) in order to buy a synagogue, which is more sacred than the square. They may sell the synagogue in order to buy an Ark, which is still more sacred. They may sell the Ark to buy coverings for the Sefer Torah. (These rules are codified in the *Shulchan Aruch, Orach Chayim* 153:2.) So it is clear from this gradation that the Ark is more sacred than the rest of the synagogue, though less sacred than the coverings of the Torah, etc.

This gradation of sanctity creates certain difficulties. How, for example, if the Ark is so sacred, do we permit incorrect *(posul)* Sefer Torahs and even other books to be kept in or near the Ark? This question and similar ones have been asked all through the legal literature, from the early scholars like Isaac Or Zorua and Asher ben Yechiel, down to the codes and the later respondents, such as Moses

Sofer (Vol. VI, 10) and others. Usually the question is put in the following form: May an old Ark, which is now too small to be used, be destroyed? May it be used (as, for example, Moses Sofer was asked) to make a coffin (the possibility of this strange-sounding question comes from the fact that the Talmud says [*Megillah* 26b] that the worn-out coverings of the Torah may be used to make shrouds for the dead).

This and similar varieties of the question of the Ark have been asked. The latest one was by David Hoffmann in his *Melamed l'Hoyil* (*Orach Chayim* #18). The question that he was asked is close to the question asked here. The congregation of Chassidim in Berlin had grown. More Sefer Torahs had been donated to it than the Ark could now contain. They were building a new Ark. Might they use the head decoration of the old Ark on the new Ark and use the rest of the old Ark as a bookcase?

In coming to a conclusion based on all this mass of material as to whether the disused Ark in question may be turned into a bookcase, we can consider the following:

1. Our present Ark does not have the sanctity mentioned in the Mishnah and the Talmud (which hold it to be even more sacred than the Sefer Torah). The Mishnah had in mind a special type of movable Ark which would be taken into the public square for fast-day services and which was made expressly to contain the Sefer Torah. But our Arks are not the movable Arks of ancient days. They are actually a cupboard built into the wall and therefore may have other objects placed in them. This argument that our present Ark does not have the old sanctity was given (as far as I know) first of all by Isaac Or Zerua (Vol. II, 386) and

cited in the Notes by Asher ben Yechiel to the chapter in *Megillah* and cited by Isserles to *Orach Chayim* 152:1. Since, as Isserles says, our present-day Ark is not exclusively an appurtenance of the Torah, as the ancient one was, we may put unfit Sefer Torahs in it, etc.

2. When a synagogue is built, the leaders of the synagogue have the right to make a precondition that all the appurtenances of the Sefer Torah, such as the Ark, etc., may be used, if necessary, for secular purposes. This rule is in *Orach Chayim* 154:8, and Isserles adds that even if it is not expressly known that this condition was made at the building of the synagogue, we may assume that it was made.

3. There is a general rule that a Sefer Torah may never be sold except for two purposes, to arrange for a marriage, and for the study of the Torah (*Megillah* 27a, *Orach Chayim* 154:6, *Yore Deah* 270:2). We may assume that the children whose class will be conducted in the synagogue premises will be taught Judaism among other subjects, and therefore we may say that they will be studying the Torah. If the sacred Torah itself may be sold for such a purpose, then surely the less sacred Ark, now disused, may be converted into a bookcase for the worthy task of teaching Torah.

6

DISPUTE OVER CANDLE-LIGHTING AND KIDDUSH

QUESTION:

In our congregation at the Friday night services, women light the Sabbath candles and the congregation remains seated; men recite the *Kiddush* and the congregation stands. A dispute has arisen on the ground that this indicates greater respect for the man's part of the service than for the woman's part of the service. Hence, it is sex discrimination. Are there clear rules as to when the congregation must stand during services? (Asked by Rabbi Stephen S. Pearce, Stamford, Connecticut.)

ANSWER:

A GENERATION AGO this question might have been dismissed as trivial and not worth serious consideration. Nowadays, however, with the nationwide agitation for women's rights, the charge of such a supposed sex discrimination could well lead to divisive disputes in many a congregation. Therefore nowadays the problem deserves full and careful consideration.

First, let us consider the general question of what tradition demands as to the places in the service where the congregation must stand. This question is not easy to answer, first, because the services are composed of many different elements which have a different legal status, and second, because the law is not always definite as to standing or sitting, and local custom varies. Perhaps it

would be helpful just to list what is fairly clear about
standing or sitting during the service.

The *Sh'ma,* the most important part of the service, may
be recited when a person is standing or walking or riding,
since it is important to recite it at its proper hour (*Orach
Chayim* 63). As for the *Shemone Esra,* standing is obliga-
tory; hence it is called the *Amida.* Not only must the
worshiper stand when he recites it, but also when the
cantor repeats it, and the people must stand (according to
the opinion of Isserles, 124:4). All agree that people
should stand when the cantor, repeating the *Shemone
Esra,* comes to the *Kedusha.* As for the reading of the
Torah, while there are strict rules against leaving the
synagogue during the reading, it is nevertheless not
required that people should stand during the reading
(146:4). At the *Duchan,* when the priest blessed the
people, it was not necessary for the people to stand (see
Be'er Hetev, Note 25 to *Orach Chayim* 128). There is also
a custom (apparently Hungarian) for the congregation to
stand while the Ark is open (cf. *Contemporary Reform
Responsa,* p. 38).

Now, specifically as to standing or sitting during the
Kiddush in the synagogue—first of all, the status of the
Kiddush as part of the public worship is in doubt. Joseph
Caro, in *Orach Chayim* 269, says the *Kiddush* properly
should be recited in the place where the meal is eaten, and
that it was inserted into the synagogue worship for the sake
of strangers who would eat in the synagogue. Since such
meals for strangers on Sabbath eve in the synagogue are no
longer provided, Caro says it would be better not to have
the *Kiddush* in the synagogue, and he calls attention to the

fact that in Eretz Yisroel they do not have the *Kiddush* in the Friday evening service at all.

However, we Ashkenazim *do* have the *Kiddush* in the synagogue on Friday evenings, and Isserles says it is the general custom to stand up for this *Kiddush* (*Orach Chayim* 269). One other dispute about standing or sitting during the *Kiddush* concerns the *Kiddush* recited in the *Succah*. This question is left undecided (*Orach Chayim* 643:2).

Now, if the status of the *Kiddush* in the synagogue is debatable, the status of blessing the Sabbath candles in the synagogue is still more debatable. There is some sort of vague precedent for it cited by Isaac Lamperonti in his *Pachad Yitzchok* under the heading of *Hadlakah*. He speaks of a custom of giving a man the privilege of kindling the two lights which will stand on the reading desk during the Friday evening service. In general, however, the lighting of the Sabbath eve candles in the synagogue is an innovation of Reform synagogues. It would be impossible for this lighting ceremony to take place in Orthodox synagogues since, especially in winter, the candles are lit after dark. While it is the especial obligation of women to light the Sabbath candles (*Orach Chayim* 263:3), men too are expected to light them when they are away from home. There is no statement that I have found anywhere as to whether those who are present at the lighting of the candles should stand or be seated.

As to the general status of women as to taking a public part in Jewish services, it must be understood that whatever participation they have today has been given them by Reform congregations. According to Orthodox law, a woman is not required to recite the daily *Sh'ma* (Mishnah *Berachos* 3:3). Authorities disagree as to whether a woman is required to recite the *Tefillah* (of course, that does not mean she is *prohibited* from reciting any of the prayers she wishes to recite), but according to the Halachic rule, she cannot discharge the obligation of the congregation by acting as cantor for prayers which she herself is not required to recite. There is an interesting note on this question in the *Be'er Hetev* to *Orach Chayim* 106:1, in which he says that most women recite their own devotions. (That is, of course, why the special *Techinnos* developed for the use of women. See my Conference paper on "Devotional Literature in the Vernacular.")

In the light of all the above complexities of law and custom, what would be the most correct and also the most practical solution to the problem which the question asked here has presented? There are two possible solutions. One is to exchange the roles of the participants; that is to say, to have a woman occasionally make *Kiddush* and a man bless the lights. Another possible solution is not to change the roles of the participants but to change the posture of the congregation, namely, that they should stand for both ceremonies or sit for both. Which of these two possible solutions is the better practically and also the more justified of the two by tradition?

The first possible solution—namely, to exchange occasionally the roles of the participants—is subject to strong objection as follows: While the legal and traditional status of *Kiddush* and candle-lighting in the *synagogue* is rather shaky and uncertain, the status of both of these ceremonies in the *home* is firmly established both in law and in custom.

After all these centuries, candle-lighting and the *Kiddush*
at home have created an almost immovable mental association in the minds of our people. It is the mother who
blesses the candles, the father who comes home from the
synagogue and makes the *Kiddush*. This is the revered
mental association in the heart of the people of Israel; and
so it is neither justified nor wise to tamper with it.

As for the second solution, it is reasonable and has
greater justification in the tradition precisely because there
is no clear rule to be derived from traditional sources, as
seen above, as to standing or sitting during either of those
two ceremonies. Therefore, we have more latitude, and
from this point of view the second solution is by far the
better. We can change the posture of the congregation and
make it identical for both ceremonies. Since there is some
inclination in the law, as mentioned above, for the people
to stand during the *Kiddush* in the synagogue, the logical
solution then would be to have the congregation stand both
for the *Kiddush* and for the candle-lighting.

May this solution be acceptable and end the controversy
in the congregation. It seems to me to be the more logical
as it is also the more justified of the two by tradition.

7

GENTILES' PART IN THE SABBATH SERVICE

QUESTION:

In our temple we have a number of mixed-marriage families who belong to the temple and attend Sabbath services. There are two parts of our Sabbath service conducted by members of the temple. One is the blessing of the Sabbath candles by a woman, and the other is the recitation of the Sabbath *Kiddush* by a man. The question, then, is this: In a mixed family, may the unconverted Gentile wife bless the Sabbath candles; and in another mixed family, may the unconverted Gentile husband recite the *Kiddush?* (Asked by Rabbi Richard Zionts, Shreveport, Louisiana.)

ANSWER:

THAT MIXED families in which one partner is unconverted to Judaism may be members of the temple is a frequent practice in many Reform congregations. The purpose of such membership is so that the couple will not be alienated and also to make it likely that the children will be raised as Jewish—and perhaps, too, so that the Gentile member, being already integrated into Jewish life, would someday wish to convert to Judaism. The only proper requirement in the case of the mixed-family synagogue membership is that the membership is in the name of the Jewish partner and only the Jewish partner would have the right to vote to determine congregational policy.

In order to make the family feel at home, many
congregations like to give the Gentile member some
participation in the service. But the question that arises is
one that is basic to the problem presented here, namely,
what part of the service is it proper for a Gentile to
conduct?

It should be stated that even in the ancient days when the
Temple stood, it was not considered strange that a Gentile
should have a share in the service. Thus we are told in the
Talmud (*Menachos* 73b) that if a Gentile brings his burnt
offerings, they are accepted and offered on the altar. It is
not only the occasional gift of a Gentile, namely, bringing
a sacrifice to the Temple, for it is also stated that if a
Gentile gives a *permanent* gift like a Menorah to the
synagogue, the gift may not be changed from the intended
purpose (i.e., and the money used for another purpose) as
long as the Gentile donor's name is remembered (*Arachin*
6b).

On the other hand, in contrast to this spiritual and ritual
hospitality, the statement is made in the Talmud (*Sanhedrin* 58b) that "a Gentile who observes the Sabbath
deserves death," and also (in *Sanhedrin* 59a) that "a
Gentile who studies the Torah deserves death."

Now at the very outset, the phrase "deserves death" is
not to be taken literally to mean that these actions
constitute a capital offense. It simply means that these
actions should positively not be permitted. This can be
seen from the statement in *Berachos* 4b, where it is said
that anybody who disagrees with the words of the Sages
deserves death. The passages refer to some *Seyag,* a
cautionary regulation of the Sages, specifically with regard

to the *Maariv* prayer. Obviously it is not a capital offense for a Jew to transgress the slightest and most minor decision of the Sages. The phrase simply means that such disobedience should not be permitted.

As for not permitting a Gentile to study the Torah, even that is not to be understood as a general proposition, because the Talmud says also (in *Sanhedrin* 59a) that a Gentile who studies the Torah becomes thereby as worthy as the High Priest himself, provided that what he studies are his God-given commandments.

The "seven commandments" are the laws of ethics and justice which God has commanded the Gentile world. When a Gentile obeys them, he is one of the "righteous Gentiles who have their portion in Paradise." This restriction, confining the Gentile's Torah study to the seven commandments, explains both prohibitions, the Gentile and the Torah and the Gentile and the Sabbath, as Maimonides states clearly in his *Hil. Melachim* 10:9, namely, that it means that it is the duty of Gentiles to obey the ethical laws which God has given them. It is not for them to add to God's decrees and obey commandments not given to them but to Israel. In other words, God's relation to mankind is expressed in two different covenants. With the Gentile world, God's covenant is the seven commandments. With Israel, God's covenant is the Torah and especially the Sabbath. Therefore Maimonides says that if a Gentile wishes to observe the Jewish Sabbath, let him become a convert and accept the special convenant which God has made with Israel.

The situation, therefore, is clear. The Sabbath is part of God's special covenant with Israel (Exodus 31:16): "The

Children of Israel shall observe the Sabbath for a perpetual covenant; a sign between Me and Israel.'' It is therefore contrary to the spirit of tradition for a Gentile to perform such parts of the service as constitute the special announcements of the Jewish-covenant Sabbath. This applies specifically to the lighting of the candles and the saying of the Sabbath *Kiddush*. The historic fact is that the Christian church publicly abolished the Sabbath for Christians and chose Sunday instead as ''the Lord's day.'' Besides this historic fact, the simple human fact is that the Jewish Sabbath can have no sacred meaning to a Christian. How, then, can he or she be permitted formally to announce its advent to Jews in a Jewish service?

Of course, the motive to make the Gentile member feel at home so as not to alienate the family is in general a good one. They can be given parts of the service to read—for example, part of the ''Old'' Testament, which is sacred to both. This is quite acceptable. The Tosefta (*Berachos* 5:21) says that if a Gentile pronounces a blessing using God's name, we say ''Amen'' to the blessing. But to have a Gentile announce the coming of the Jewish Sabbath to a Jewish congregation is contrary to the spirit of Jewish tradition.

8

CEMETERY WORK ON ROSH HASHONAH

QUESTION:

Our cemetery needs to have a deep well dug. This is an expensive enterprise and the contract for it has been let. For technical reasons, the work in digging the well, once it is started, must be continuous. This will bring the work through Rosh Hashonah. Is this permitted? (Asked by Louis J. Freehof, San Francisco, California.)

ANSWER:

SINCE THE digging of the well will take many weeks, it will also include the likelihood of work on a number of Sabbaths. The New Year is a *Yom Tov,* and the laws of Sabbath work are even stricter than the laws of *Yom Tov.* For example, cooking for the family may be done on *Yom Tov* and may not be done on the Sabbath. Therefore the question should really read as follows: May this cemetery work be done on the Sabbath and holiday? It should be clear that if, for some reason, it is permitted on the Sabbath, it will all the more be permissible on the holiday.

The assumption is that the firm contracted to dig the well is not a Jewish firm but a Gentile one. If it were a Jewish firm, the owners would be absolutely prohibited by Jewish law from work on the Sabbath and the holiday. So we must assume it is a Gentile firm which has the contract, and the question, therefore, really is: May a Gentile firm work in behalf of a Jewish institution on the Sabbath and holidays?

Generally it is forbidden by Jewish law for a Jew to give orders to a Gentile to work for him on the Sabbath and holidays. Then how is it possible to employ a Gentile, as many synagogues and households do, to put out the lights on the Sabbath? The answer is that it is forbidden to *tell* the Gentile to put out the lights since he is your agent and he is working for you on your orders on the Sabbath. The presumption is that the Gentile in these cases knows of his own accord what to do, and he does it without a direct order from the Jew to have him do work for him on the Sabbath.

Therefore, it would seem that work by a Gentile firm would be forbidden on the Sabbath and holidays, but that is not actually so. It depends on the nature of the contract made with the Gentile firm. The Talmud has detailed descriptions of many types of contracts, a number of them pertaining to various types of sharecropping. Out of the Talmudic laws on contracts, the great twelfth-century authority, Rabbenu Tam, Rashi's grandson, derived the principle called *kablonus*. This means literally "acceptance," but more fully it means a contract of a special type. If it were a contract to pay the Gentile or his workmen every day for the day's work, then it would be forbidden for the Gentile or his workmen to work on the Sabbath because we would be paying specifically for Sabbath work in our behalf.

But *kablonus* is not a wage-contract but a total job-contract. The Gentile firm is engaged to do the whole job for a certain sum, and it is entirely the Gentile's decision whether to work by day or by night or what days to work and what days not to work. In that case, by a *kablonus* contract the Gentile firm may work on the Sabbath or holidays because it is its own decision and the Jew does not get any specific benefit from the work on the Sabbath. He is paying for the *whole* job, and it is the Gentile who decides when to work and when not to work. This decision of Rabbenu Tam—that Gentiles working on a *kablonus* contract (i.e., a job-contract) may work for a Jew on the Sabbath—is given by Rabbenu Tam in two places, in the *Tosfos* to *Zora* 21b and also in *Sabbath* 17b.

Some scholars tend to disagree with Rabbenu Tam, mostly on the following ground: If the Gentile is carrying out the building contract in the city, where Jewish people see the work done on Sabbath and holiday, they may not know that it is a *kablonus* contract and may think that the Jew has made a daily wage-contract and, therefore, is violating the Sabbath. Hence the law to satisy these objections is stated as follows (in the *Tur* and in the *Shulchan Aruch, Orach Chayim* 244:1): that a Gentile on a *kablonus* contract may work on the Sabbath, but some believe that in a public place where (Jewish) people pass, he may not do so.

Now it happens that this work is being done in the cemetery, where people generally do not walk around, and where no funerals are held on Sabbath and New Year, and where people do not visit the cemetery on those days. Therefore there is no objection at all to this type of work.

To sum up: A *kablonus* contract with a Gentile leaves the contractor free to decide which days to work. Hence the Jew does not get any specific benefit for Sabbath or holiday work, and does not give any order for this kind of work. Also, on the days in question people do not visit the cemetery. Hence there is no objection in Jewish law to the Gentile contractor working on those days.

9

TITLES IN MEMORIAL LIST

QUESTION:

It has been the practice in the congregation that when reading the *Yahrzeit* lists, the titles of the deceased, such as "doctor," "rabbi," have been used. Some objection has been raised to this on the ground that it is contrary to the Jewish spirit of equality in death. What is Jewish tradition in this matter? (Asked by Rabbi Judea B. Miller, Rochester, New York.)

ANSWER:

THERE IS no doubt that the tendency of our tradition has been to increase equality in all matters relating to death, burial, etc. A famous Chassidic rabbi of the last generation, Eliezer Spiro (Der Muncaczer), objects to flowers at the funerals precisely on the ground that richer people would have more flowers and poorer people would have fewer flowers or none at all, and therefore that the use of flowers at funerals is for this reason (among other reasons) not to be permitted at Jewish funerals. We, in modern congregations, permit the use of flowers even though we know that what Rabbi Spiro objected to will actually take place. Rich or prominent people will have a much more ostentatious and beautiful flower display at the funeral than would poor or humble people. Nevertheless, in spite of our permitting this difference, our motivation in general is in

accord with Jewish tradition that we do try to achieve a
sense of equality in these matters.

We in liberal congregations would not be as absolute in
such matters as are the Orthodox, who, for example, use a
plain wooden coffin for everybody, whereas we would
permit a family to have a more expensive casket than
another. With us, therefore, the question is not an absolute
one. We would ask, *how much* equality should there be,
and how much latitude should we permit in the direction of
differences between one funeral and another?

I was recently asked whether or not at all funerals a plain
blanket should be used to conceal the coffin during the
services. In this way the differences between expensive
and inexpensive caskets would not be observed by the
congregation. The conclusion we came to on that question
will have some bearing on the problem before us. It was to
this effect: We should not be too strict about such matters
and such observances which are transient or which disap-
pear from permanent view. The expensive coffin is buried
and becomes as invisible as the plain wooden one. The
flowers fade away. However, the tombstone remains
visible permanently. Therefore the congregation should
not permit too much ornateness in this permanent type of
memorial. As a matter of fact, many historic Orthodox
congregations supervise the tombstones to prevent certain
ones being overelaborate or conspicuous (cf. Greenwald,
Kol Bo, p. 380).

Nevertheless, it is to be noted that as far as the names on
the tombstones are concerned, certain distinctions were
permitted and, in fact, were in general practice. A rabbi
was certainly given his rabbinical title. Every Kohen's

tombstone was marked by the hands open in priestly blessing. And even the Levites had their graves marked by an incised pitcher of water, because the Levites poured water on the hands of the priests before they blessed the people. So we see that even with such a permanent object as a tombstone, a certain amount of distinction was permitted and, indeed, customary in Orthodox cemeteries.

The situation, then, in Jewish tradition is as follows: The general attitude toward equality is mitigated by latitude toward certain reasonable distinctions. In other words, the ideal of equality is, in practice, far from absolute. In the light of the above, what rule should govern the reading of the names in the memorial list? Should it be just the name or should it be the name with its customary title? The question really is, are these titles a public declaration of special honor given to certain individuals? As a matter of fact, these titles are not at all a mark of publicly announced privilege. They represent merely a special function in the community, and the title has become a part of the name. We do not assume by our use of the term that we declare that a doctor is more to be honored than a businessman. We are simply describing a social function.

However, since the question *has* arisen, there must be some feeling in the congregation that the title *is* a mark of special honor and therefore should not be used. How, then, should we proceed in this matter in the face of these objections? We must decide it as many problems have been decided in the law, namely by analogy. An analogous discussion has arisen in the responsa of the last generation with regard to memorial lists. The question with regard to the lists was whether the names of the deceased should be read, each one separately, and the *Mi Sheberach* or the prayer *El Mole Rachamim* should be recited separately in behalf of each person, or should the whole list be read in sequence and one prayer be uttered for them all? (This is more or less our custom.) The question is discussed, for example, by Eliezer Deutsch in *Pri Hasedy,* Vol. I, #79; by Shrage Tennenbaum in his *Neta Shorek, Orach Chayim* 8; and by Jacob Tennenbaum in his *Naharey Afarsimon, Choshen Mishpot, #5.*

The conclusion reached by Jacob Tennenbaum is based on the question of the special honor due to a rabbi (*Yore Deah* 242:2, in Isserles) namely, that if the local rabbi has not yet been consulted on a certain question, then another rabbi may be consulted. But if the local rabbi has already been consulted, it is not permitted to offend the local rabbi by consulting another rabbi. On the basis of this analogy, Tennenbaum concludes as to the listing of the memorial names as follows: If there is already an established custom in the community to have a separate prayer for each name, this custom should not be changed, because to change it now would be dishonor to the departed. But if there is no such established custom, then the names may be read in one consecutive list.

This, then, may well be our conclusion here. We should follow the established custom in the community. If hitherto the names were used with the title and now the custom would be changed and the titles omitted from now on, this could be deemed a deprecation of those honored dead who in past years were named with their titles. If, however, there is no such established custom, the congregation need not change and from now on *add* the title. In other words, if the custom of using the titles has been followed until now, this custom need not be changed because it cannot be considered objectionable to Jewish tradition, in spite of the general Jewish tendency for equality in all such matters.

10

SUCCAH AND ARTIFICIAL FRUIT

QUESTION:

Is it permissible to have artificial fruit as decorations for the *Succah?* The advantage of artificial fruit would be that it does not spoil quickly and can be used year after year. (Asked by Rabbi Richard A. Zionts, Shreveport, Louisiana.)

ANSWER:

OF COURSE, Succos being harvest time, it is natural to decorate the *Succah* with fruits which are readily available, apples, pears, etc., and in fact, this is the general and natural custom. But would it be permitted to use artificial fruits because of the advantages mentioned in the question?

The question amounts to this: Did they ever use anything but real fruit as decoration, and is real fruit actually required? What laws there are concerning the decorations generally deal with the question whether these fruits may be eaten during Succos, or are they a part of the *Succah* and must they remain as such until the festival is over? (*Shulchan Aruch, Orach Chayim* 638:2).

Nevertheless, while the obvious custom and the law about eating the decorations indicate that real fruit was used, there are some indications that other types of decoration were used. Thus, for example, in the Palestinian Talmud (*Succah* 51b) there is a discussion as to the height that the *Succah* must have, and the specific question is whether the decorations may be counted as diminishing the height or not. On that question the Talmud says that if the decorations are of the sort suitable for the *Succah* covering *(schach),* then they may be said to diminish the height of the *Succah*. What is meant by "suitable for the *Succah* covering"? It means vegetable matter, branches, etc. Then this would indicate that the decorations need not necessarily be vegetable matter at all since the Talmud asks "*if* it is." As a matter of fact, Epstein in *Aruch Ha-Shulchan* makes this distinction quite clear. In discussing the law which forbids the eating of the decorations, he says, "*If* the decorations are food, i.e., edible, they may not be taken down and used during Succos" (*Orach Chayim* 638:10).

But we do not need to rely entirely on this negative inference. As a matter of fact, we have positive statements that non-edibles were used for *Succah* decorations. Maharil (14th century), speaking of the decorations of the *Succah,* says, "Praiseworthy is the custom of the Ashkenaz that we spread beautiful cloths (tapestries) as decorations of the *Succah*." And in fact Isserles, in his note to *Orach Chayim* 638:2, also speaks of the custom of decorating the *Succah* with hangings of handsome cloths.

Therefore, although there is no mention of artificial fruit (it may be they did not know of such), nevertheless the law is clear that they used decorations that were not edible (at least on the walls of the *Succah*). Therefore we may well conclude that there is no clear or real objection to the suggested use of artificial fruit.

11

LULAV AND ESROG AFTER SUCCOS

QUESTION:

Is there any guidance in the legal tradition as to how one should dispose of the *lulav* and *esrog* after Succos is over? (Asked by Rabbi Mark Staitman, Pittsburgh, Pennsylvania.)

ANSWER:

IT IS VIRTUALLY impossible to preserve a *lulav* and *esrog* for another year. The *esrog* dries up, and the leaves of the *lulav* dry up and grow brittle. So the normal procedure has always been to get new *esrogim* and *lulavim* each year for Succos. This is the reason for the question which has been asked here, as to what is the proper mode of disposal of this year's *esrog* and *lulav* after Succos is over.

In our religious life there is a large variety of objects must be removed when a larger Ark is needed, coverings of the Sefer Torah, mantles, etc., which get worn out, fringes *(tzitzis)* which get torn, etc. Therefore it is understandable that there has developed a great deal of law on the question of proper disposal of such objects when they are no longer usable.

It must be understood at the outset that these various objects are not all of equal sanctity. Some are much holier than others. So the Mishnah (in *Megillah* 3:1) discusses the necessary procedure when a community sells the public square. The square had a sort of a semi-sanctity because services were held there on fast-days. When the square is sold, we must use the money to buy a synagogue. When a synagogue is sold, we may buy an Ark with the money. When an Ark is sold, we may buy Torah covers with the money. When the Torah covers are sold, we may buy Torahs, etc. In other words, there is an ascending scale of sanctity, and in the case of sale of any of these objects, we always step upward in the order of sanctity, but never downward.

All this applies, of course, when there is an actual sale of these sacred objects. But what if there is no sale at all, but the sacred object was merely worn out and must be discarded, as happens with the mantle on the Torah or the Torah itself? What then should be done with them? This brings us close to the question which has been asked.

With regard to sacred objects which are no longer usable, and also with regard to objects which have already fulfilled their religious purpose, such as torn fringes or *tzitzis* or the walls of the *Succah* after Succos is over, the law makes a sharp distinction between two classes of such objects. One class is called "appurtenances of holiness" *(tashmishey kedusha)*. The other class is called "appurtenances of a *mitzvah*" *(tashmishey mitzvah)*. In the former class, the worn-out object retains its sanctity even when no longer in use. In the second class, after the object has been used in the performance of the *mitzvah*, it has no sanctity left at all. See the statement of Joseph Caro with regard to the broken fringes in *Orach Chayim* 21:1 *(en b'gufa*

kedusha). Included in the former class, the "appurtenances of holiness," are unused Sefer Torahs, coverings
of the Sefer Torahs, *tefillin, mezuzahs,* etc. These objects,
though now unusable, are still sacred and are to be hidden
away *(nignozin).* Of course, "hidden away" may include
burial in the cemetery.

The second class, objects which are no longer sacred
after having served their purpose, includes the *Succah*
itself, fringes torn off a *tallis,* the *lulav,* etc. These objects
need not even be stored away but, as the Talmud says, they
may be simply thrown away ("on the dunghill") (cf.
Orach Chayim 21:1, see the whole discussion in *Megillah*
26b).

One might mention here that printed prayerbooks,
which could well be considered merely "appurtenances of
a *mitzvah*" and therefore be thrown away when they
become worn out, nevertheless are stored and often buried
(even torn pages from old prayerbooks), as are the
"appurtenances of holiness," but that is because they
contain the Name of God on almost every page.

The list in the Talmud of "appurtenances of *mitzvah*"
which may be thrown away includes the *lulav* but does not
mention the *esrog.* It is obvious, however, that the *esrog*
also belongs to this class which has no more sanctity once
it has served its purpose (i.e., *tashmishey mitzvah*). The
proof of this is the fact that the *esrog,* being edible, was
eaten after it had served its purposes of the *mitzvah.* So the
Talmud speaks of the eating of the citron by children and
by adults (*Succah* 46a), and the *Shulchan Aruch* states that
in Israel *esrogim* may be eaten after Shemini Atzeres, but
outside of Israel, not until after the ninth day.

In passing, a folkloristic use of the citron might also be mentioned here. It was a widespread folk-custom that pregnant women on Hoshana Rabba would bite off the bitter stem of the *esrog,* the reason being as follows: In *Midrash Rabba (Genesis R.* 15:7) there are many speculations as to what was the species of fruit with which Eve sinned in the Garden of Eden, and one opinion is that the forbidden fruit was the *esrog.* So the pregnant women bite the *bitter* part of the esrog in order to declare that they do not share in Eve's sin and thus hope to earn God's protection during pregnancy and childbirth (see the explanation of this folk custom in Hershovitz, *Ozar Minhagim,* p. 113).

Thus it is clear that the *lulav* and the *esrog* have no sacredness at all left in them after having been used in the *mitzvah* on Succos and thus can be disposed of off-hand. But one can easily understand how later tradition felt uneasy about treating so cavalierly objects which just a short time ago were revered as sacred during the perform-ance of the *mitzvah.* Therefore folk-custom began to add precautions as to the mode of disposal of these objects. For example, the torn threads of the fringes were used by Maharil *(Be'er Hetev)* as bookmarks (cf. *Be'er Hetev* to *Shulchan Aruch, Orach Chayim* 21). As for the willows used on Hoshana Rabba, the note *Haga'ha* to Asher ben Yechiel to *Megillah,* Chapter IV, states that while the willows may be thrown away, they should not be trodden underfoot. And it is reported by Maharil that pious people often save the willows to light the fire later for the baking of the *matzos.* Thus, though discarded, they were still used for a *mitzvah* (cf. Isserles to *Orach Chayim* 664:9).

In the light of the traditional disinclination just to throw away these objects carelessly (which would be completely permissible), we may come to the following conclusion. Strictly speaking, the *lulav* and *esrog* may indeed just be thrown away ("on the dunghill"). But we would share the feelings of the past that it would be wrong to see them lying on a heap of debris in a public thoroughfare. Therefore they should be disposed of with some respect to the status which, though they now lack, they once had. They should perhaps be wrapped up carefully, so as not to be visible to any passerby, and then put away for disposal or, since when Succos is over furnaces are soon lit, they may be perhaps burned up in the furnace. This would be a decent disposal which many authorities permit even for disused prayerbook pages (see references in *Reform Responsa*, pp. 71 ff.).

12

A GLASS MEZUZAH

QUESTION:

An artisan made a *mezuzah* case of spun glass. In this case the written *mezuzah* was inserted and rolled in such a way that the writing of the text is visible. Is this type of *mezuzah* in accordance with the law and the tradition? (Asked by Vigdor W. Kavaler, Pittsburgh, Pennsylvania.)

ANSWER:

THERE IS NO law that would forbid a *mezuzah* case made of glass. As a matter of fact, the *Shulchan Aruch* indicates that the case may be of *any* material. In *Yore Deah* 289:1 it is stated that the written text be placed in a case of reeds or *any material.*

Nor is there any basic objection if part of the writing in the *mezuzah* is visible through the glass. As a matter of fact, it is a long-established custom to have one or two inscriptions on the back of the text, and these inscriptions should be visible. There is, first of all, the custom that the word *Shaddai,* "The Almighty," should be visible (see *Yore Deah* 288:14). And also there is a coded phrase which is also meant to be visible. The phrase is *Kuzu b'muchtsas kuzu.* These words have no meaning in themselves but are a coded form of the words in the *mezuzah, Adonoi Elohenu Adonoi.* The key to the code is a simple one. The words are made up by using the next letter of the alphabet. Instead of the *Yod* of *Adonoi,* the next letter in the alphabet, *Kaf,* is used; instead of the next letter, *Hey,* of *Adonoi,* the next letter of the alphabet, *Vav,* is used; and so on to produce the coded formula. This coded phrase, together with *Shaddai,* is meant to be seen. So there can be no general objection to words being visible through the glass.

But in the case of this specific *mezuzah* there *is* a strong objection. The *mezuzah* text in this glass case is rolled in a way that the text of the Biblical passage used in the *mezuzah* is on the outside. This is absolutely wrong. The two phrases mentioned above that are to be seen are on the back, the blank side, of the text. The text itself must be rolled so as to be inward and not visible. It must be rolled up beginning at the back of the lines and rolled toward the front so that only the blank back, except for the two phrases mentioned, is visible. To roll it as in this *mezuzah* with the text *outside* is absolutely wrong (see *Yore Deah* 288:14).

I must reexamine the glass *mezuzah* to see whether or not the glass is fused in such a way as to seal the *mezuzah* inside the case so that it is immovable. If that is the fact, then this *mezuzah* is wrong on this second count also; because it is a rule that Sefer Torahs and *tefillin* and *mezuzahs* must be regularly inspected. A *mezuzah* must be inspected at least once in seven years (*Yore Deah* 291:1). If a *mezuzah* is not removable from the case, it cannot be inspected, and therefore the law is violated in this regard.

To sum up, then, there is no objection to the *mezuzah* case being of glass. If the *mezuzah* is rolled properly—

namely, with the writing of the text *inside,* and not visible from the outside—and if the case is so constructed that the text can be removed for periodical inspection, then this *mezuzah* is quite proper for use.

13

THE SIGNS OF THE ZODIAC ON SYNAGOGUE
WINDOWS

QUESTION:

Is it proper to have the twelve signs of the zodiac on the
stained-glass windows of our temple? The status of the
twelve symbols in Jewish tradition is somewhat vague, and
so there could be arguments for or against their use. What we
need, therefore, is the preponderance of attitude or opinion
on whether to use them or not. (Asked by Rabbi Albert A.
Michels, Sun City, Arizona.)

ANSWER:

FIRST OF all, the argument *against* their use: One motive
for putting the signs of the zodiac on the windows might be
for the purpose (even incidentally for the purpose) of
holding the interest of those people nowadays who believe
in astrology. If this is the motive, then it is absolutely
against Jewish tradition. The objection to astrology stems
from the verse in Jeremiah 10:2: "Thus saith the Lord:
Learn not the way of the nations, and be not dismayed at
the signs of heaven; for the nations are dismayed at them."
On this verse the Talmud in *Shabbat* 156a says: No
constellation governs the life of Israel *(eyn mazol l'Yisroel)*. In other words, all the astrology which was so
elaborately developed by the Babylonians is forbidden to
us.

However, if the intention and the effect is not to encourage the belief in astrology, then much can be said in favor of having the signs of the zodiac on the windows. The signs of the zodiac are taken to represent the twelve tribes of Israel. Furthermore, each of the signs is given a religious significance in the Midrashic literature. Thus Aries the lamb is the pure sacrifice of Isaac, etc. (see the article "Zodiac" in the *Jewish Encyclopedia* and in the new *Encyclopaedia Judaica*).

There is also a more direct reason for permitting the use of these signs on the windows. In the older Halachah, most of the objection against decorations on synagogue walls and in prayerbooks was based upon the fear that they would distract the people from their prayers (see the reference in *Modern Reform Responsa,* pp. 185 ff.). But the signs of the zodiac were actually printed in all the holiday prayerbooks for the rain and dew prayers on Succos and Passover. If, therefore, the signs of the zodiac were printed in the prayerbook for the people to look at *when* they pray, then surely it was deemed even praiseworthy to have them.

Our answer, therefore, must be on balance. If you believe that the effect of the pictures of the signs of the zodiac will encourage interest in astrology, then it is wrong to have them. But if there is no such concern or danger, then there is plenty of tradition in favor of having them.

14

CIRCUMCISING THE CHILD OF AN UNMARRIED COUPLE

QUESTION:

An unmarried couple living together have had a male child. They ask that this child be circumcised and all the usual public announcements be made in the congregation. (Asked by Rabbi Jonathan M. Brown, Long Beach, California.)

ANSWER:

IT IS NOT clear from the question whether both the man and the woman are Jewish or whether the woman is a married woman (i.e., to a man other than the man she is now living with). If she is a Jewish woman, the child is Jewish whether the man is Jewish or not. If she is an unmarried Jewess, the child is both Jewish and legitimate. If she is a Jewish married woman, the child is illegitimate, a *mamzer*.

Even if the child is illegitimate, he has every right pertaining to a legitimate Jewish child. He may be Bar Mitzvah, etc. (see references in *Contemporary Reform Responsa,* p. 92). Certainly he must be circumcised (see *Shulchan Aruch, Yore Deah* 265:4). It is to be noticed, however, that the *Shulchan Aruch,* in discussing the circumcision of an illegitimate child, gives two cautions: first, that the concluding blessing of the child be omitted, and second (according to Isserles), it must be publicly announced that the child is a *mamzer*. The reason for the first caution—that the blessing be omitted—is explained by the *Shach:* we do not want such children to increase in the Jewish community; the reason for the second caution is that a *mamzer,* while he has every right as a Jew, has one disability—namely, he may not marry into a legitimate Jewish family. Hence the need for the public announcement that the child is a *mamzer.*

It is debatable whether in our contemporary mood we would follow these two cautions of the *Shulchan Aruch,* but we learn from the very fact that such cautions were required that we, too, even in our contemporary permissive mood, also have strong reason for caution. Would we want to make public announcement to our congregation that we consider such living together to be equivalent to marriage? Are we not justified and in duty bound to indicate in some way or other our opposition, from the standpoint of Judaism and public morality, to such so-called meaningful relationships?

We certainly must be concerned with how "meaningful" such a relationship is meant to be. Does the couple mean it to be lifelong, as every marriage should be intended to be, or is it just a sexual convenience in which both parties hold themselves free to leave each other without any formalities? There is no law, Jewish or public, to put any hindrance to their just leaving each other at the slightest quarrel or impulse. If this couple considers their relationship a sort of enduring marriage, there is indeed something in the Jewish past that would apparently justify it. The first Mishnah in *Kiddushin* says that a woman may be married by the very act of sexual intercourse. But this is understood to mean that the man intends this sexual act to mean marriage, i.e., permanent. In fact, some authorities require that the actual intention of the act be solemnly declared in the presence of witnesses. However, this marriage by the symbolic sexual act *(b' biya)* was frowned upon; Rav in Babylon publicly whipped anyone who presumed to marry in this way (see *Kiddushin* 76b), and his reason was to discourage public immorality *(m' shum peritsusa)*. In other words, even if such a couple means their relationship to be relatively permanent, it is still destructive of public morality, and we must surely follow the intention of Rav and discountenance it and discourage it as much as possible.

This, then, brings us to the question of the circumcision of the child. The child has every right to circumcision, but we have every duty to follow certain cautions in this situation in order to discourage such a relationship. I do not think that in our present mood we would feel required, if the child is illegitimate, to make a public declaration of the fact. It is not our feeling today to stigmatize any innocent child, and as for the danger that an illegitimate child might perhaps marry into a legitimate family, we do not care to keep close watch upon such possibilities. We do not seek to discover whether some illegitimate has married into any particular family. In other words, we follow the Talmud in *Kiddushin* 76b, where the Sages say, ''All Jewish families are presumed to be legitimate.''

Our concern is not with the child but with the parents. Our responsibility is to indicate our disapproval of such a relationship and certainly not to declare that we consider such a relationship as normal and proper as that of a regularly married couple. Therefore the suggestion of the questioner is sound, "We would certainly attend and officiate at a circumcision or naming that would be privately conducted, but would prefer not to follow our normal procedure of naming the child during a Sabbath service because of the parents' unmarried state."

In other words, we transfer the traditional cautions from the child to the parents. The child will have every right, but the couple cannot receive public acknowledgment or honor from a Jewish congregation.

15

KIDNEY TRANSPLANTS

QUESTION:

One of two sisters in middle life needs a kidney transplant. The doctors prefer to implant a kidney from a close relative (such as a sister) because the similarities of the bodies will make the danger of the rejection of the kidney by the recipient's body much less likely. Is the healthy sister ethically or legally in duty bound, according to the Halachah, to donate her kidney to her sister? Also, is the sick sister entitled to demand that donation? The problem is complicated by the fact that the two sisters are not on friendly terms. (Asked by Rabbi David Polish, Chicago, Illinois.)

ANSWER:

As FAR AS the ethics of the Halachah is concerned, this question goes back to the Biblical verse in Leviticus 19:16: "Stand not idly by the [shedding of the] blood of thy neighbor." The Talmud (in *Sanhedrin* 73a) makes this general command more specific and says: If you see your neighbor drowning in the river or being attacked by robbers and you do not come to his help, you have violated the Biblical mandate, "Stand not idly by."

The post-Talmudic scholars realize that the Talmud is not specific as to just how much the potential rescuer is in duty bound to endanger himself. The post-Talmudic discussions on this question revolve around the question whether the victim is in real and *imminent* danger or only in *potential* danger *(s'fak pikuach nefesh),* and as to the potential rescuer, whether he would put himself in immi-

62

nent danger or only in potential danger. These alternatives are discussed, and the general conclusion is that the potential rescuer must exert all means by the expenditure of money (example: hiring people to overcome the robbers, etc.) but is *not* in duty bound to put *himself* in serious physical danger.

Recently there has developed a good deal of Halachic discussion and decision as to how this interpreted Talmudic dictum applies to the specific problem of kidney transplants. Most of this discussion is connected with the historic Orthodox hospital in Jerusalem, Shaare Zedek. This hospital maintains a scholar whose task it is to study all the modern medical problems in the light of the Halachah. This scholar is Eliezer Waldenberg, whose responsa works *(Tzitz Eliezer)* have reached thirteen volumes. In addition to this monumental work of Eliezer Waldenberg, many of the physicians connected with the hospital are themselves Halachic scholars, and they have developed an ongoing symposium on all the new medical-Halachic questions. They publish these symposia in a series called ''Healing'' *(Assia)*. Thus we are now fortunate in having a considerable body of decisions on questions such as the one asked here and on other new questions, such as artificial insemination, heart transplants, life-maintaining machinery, etc.

As to our question here, Eliezer Waldenberg has two responsa. The more important one is in Volume X, #7. In this responsum he cites a responsum from David ben Zimri, who was brought as a child from Spain in 1492, became rabbi of Egypt, and after he reached the age of ninety, left Egypt and continued his rabbinate in Safed. In the responsa of David ben Zimri *(Radbaz)*, Vol. III, #625, he discusses a question which may have had actual reality under the rule of the Egyptian pashas. It is as follows: The ruler tells a certain Jew that he is going to kill another Jew unless this (first) Jew allows him to cut off his arm or his leg. The question, then, is as follows: Is a man required by Jewish law to sacrifice one of his own limbs to save another person, a question which, of course, comes close to our question about kidney transplants. *Radbaz* decides that while one is in duty bound to do what one can to save one's neighbor, one is not in duty bound to endanger his own life (as might well happen with the crude amputation surgery of those days). In fact, says *Radbaz,* if he does indeed risk his life to save the other man, he is just being foolishly righteous *(chasid shota).* This in effect becomes the present-day decision of Waldenberg. He says that one is not in duty bound to risk his own life in order possibly to save another. As for the case cited by *Radbaz,* we do not actually know what the outcome would have been—after the first Jew had given up his limb, the pasha might nevertheless have killed the Jew whose life he had threatened. Similarly, we are not sure that the kidney transplant will be successful. Thus this would be a case of a person risking his life for the *potential* (not sure) saving of another.

After deciding that a man is not required by Jewish ethics to risk his own life for the potential saving of another life, Waldenberg moves on to a further question, namely, that not only is the potential donor not *required* to give his kidney, but it may even be said that he is really *forbidden* to do so, since, as Waldenberg indicates, we are not the absolute masters of our own body. Actually one's body is a God-given !oan to us, and we have no right seriously to harm it. In support of this latter idea, he quotes the *Shulchan Aruch* of Schneir Zalman of Ladi, who says (in *Sh'miras Ha-Guf* #14), "You are in duty bound to protect your body and do it no harm."

However, Waldenberg himself somewhat mitigates this completely negative conclusion. He considers the probability of some future changes in the situation, based on the possibility of medical progress. If, he says, medical science so advances in the future that the danger to the donor is largely eliminated and the likelihood of benefit to the donee is greatly enhanced, then such a gift of the kidney may be permitted, provided the potential giver does it of his own complete and full-hearted free-will.

This subject is further discussed in the symposium *Assia* mentioned above. There the physicians have a somewhat more permissive attitude than Eliezer Waldenberg, being more confident of the success of the surgical procedures involved. In the complete Volume I, p. 186, there is an article by Professor Kahn, who says that of course the donation has a better chance for success if the kidney is from a close relative, but the kidney may only be taken from him "if he in truth wishes to give it from the depth of his heart and has no hesitation or limitations to his intention."

Of course, if the donor has serious doubts about giving up his kidney, or has to be too heavily persuaded to do so, then, as Waldenberg says, if some damage occurs through the operation, the doctor or those who persuaded the donor are the ones who have incurred guilt.

Applying all this to the specific question asked, we can say that if the sister who is asked to give the kidney is not completely willing to do so, it is against Jewish ethics to try too insistently to persuade her. After all, the operation on the potential donor to remove the kidney involves danger and may not go well, and also the operation of implanting it may not be quite successful, and it is clear that Jewish ethics does not require us to enter into potential personal danger, especially when the benefit of the one to be rescued is itself not absolutely certain.

16

THE HOSPICE

QUESTION:

In 1967, an English doctor, Cecily Saunders, opened a new sort of institution which was called St. Christopher's Hospice. The basic purpose of the hospice was to ease the process of dying for terminal patients. The hospice proved so popular that similar institutions and organizations with the same motivation have spread rapidly across the United States. The question has now been raised whether the motivations and the methods of the hospice idea are in conformity with the spirit of Jewish legal tradition. (Asked by Sonia Syme, Detroit, Michigan.)

ANSWER:

A DISCUSSION of this question involves an analysis of the motivation for the hospice as an institution and a movement and its relationship to present medical practice with regard to a terminal patient. Dr. Saunders, herself a practicing physician and undoubtedly working in hospitals, had come to the conclusion, with which many now agree, that a hospital is not the proper place for a dying patient. A hospital is primarily directed to the task of curing a curable patient. So, for example, certain practices directed to the task of curing are followed in a hospital. The patient, when needed, receives all sorts of medicines, injections, and is often attached to various tubes, etc.

Also, in general, visiting by relatives and friends is kept to a minimum. All this is deemed by the hospital to be necessary to the process of curing and is, therefore, quite justified.

But suppose it has become clear that the patient cannot be cured. Even so, the hospital practice in dealing with this incurable patient will tend to follow the practice used for a curable patient. There will be a continuation of the chemotherapy and tubes and electrical machines as if the patient could still be cured. Also, the patient is still kept relatively isolated from his family and thus often dies in loneliness, even though this isolation was no longer necessary, since no cure was possible. Therefore, because hospitals tend to follow with the incurable the methods for the curable, Dr. Saunders established, one might say, a special sort of hospital, one specifically for the dying. It is a bright building where relatives come as often as they wish. The patient, of course, gets medical relief for pain, but above all, he spends his last weeks surrounded by his dear ones and is allowed to die in dignity.

The hospice idea has spread in the United States. But so far there are only one or two special buildings provided for this purpose. Mostly there are, in most American cities, organizations devoted to the essential hospice idea, namely, that the dying patient is allowed (as it is believed) to die in dignity, helped and consoled by the presence of his or her dear ones, and without being forced to undergo such medical treatments as are no longer necessary. Also, there will be religious and psychiatric help for the patient, providing him or her with the mental and emotional means to face the inevitable end with equanimity. This is the aim which is now sought for in institutions or through the hospice idea in the dying patient's home. Even in the original institution, St. Christopher's in London, the patients spend most of the time at home. The question now is, what is the attitude of Judaism to this idea and method?

The first question that concerns us is this: How does the patient know that his case is terminal? If part of the hospice idea is to inform the patient that he is no longer curable and that he is dying, and this is the first step in the hospice process, then it must be stated at the very outset that to tell a patient that there is no longer any hope for cure, even if this is a fact, is contrary to the spirit of Judaism. We are told in the Talmud *(Berachos* 10a) that when King Hezekiah was sick, Isaiah said to him, ''Put your house in order because you are going to die.'' But Hezekiah rejected this dire prophecy and said, ''I have it as tradition from my father's house [i.e., David's] that even if a sword is hanging above a man's head, he should not give up hope for deliverance.'' As a matter of fact, Isaiah's prediction that Hezekiah's case was terminal proved to be wrong, and King Hezekiah recovered. This idea of not telling a patient that he is going to die finds its expression in Jewish law *(Yore Deah* 338). If, for example, we ask a terminal patient to make confession of his sins (based on *b. Shabbat* 32a), we must reassure him by saying, ''Many make confession and do not die.'' Furthermore, we do not suggest confession in the presence of ignorant people or of women and children, lest they burst into tears and sadden the dying man. The exact words used are ''lest they weep and break his heart'' (based on the *Tur,* ibid.). No coffin must be brought where the patient will see it. No weeping relatives must be allowed in his presence (cf. *Tur,* ibid.). However, we may assume that in modern times a patient does not have to be told outright that his case is hopeless. He generally gets to know it in one way or another. So we may well assume that the hospice will not need to tell the patient that he is going to die, but is dealing with patients who already know that they will not recover.

Now the purpose of the hospice is to change the hospital practice of keeping the patient undisturbed and alone, except, of course, for the reluctant permission given to the closest relatives. Instead, the hospice encourages the family to be present through all the terminal stages. This idea that the dying should not die alone is fully in accordance with Jewish law. The *Shulchan Aruch* states (in *Yore Deah* 339:4) that when a person is dying, it is actually forbidden to leave his presence, so that his soul should not leave him while he is alone. See, also, Isserles, who says that it is actually a *mitzvah* to be in the presence of the patient as he is dying, and Moshe Rifkes, in his *Be'er Hagolah,* says that the purpose of this is that the person should not die in a state of sorrow. In other words, the idea of the hospice that there is consolation in the presence of dear ones and friends at the time of dying is an idea which is fully in accord with Jewish tradition.

As for the final purpose of the hospice—that a dying patient should not be subjected to all the tubes and other methods which prevent him from dying, but which cannot possibly prevent his death but only delay it—all such forcibly keeping of the dying patient alive is contrary to Jewish tradition. A man has the right to die in dignity. (See all the references involved in this question in *Modern Reform Responsa,* pp. 197 ff., the responsum entitled "Allowing a Terminal Patient to Die.")

To sum up, then, it would be contrary to the spirit of

Jewish law to tell any patient that there is no hope and that he is going to die. However, if the patient already knows this, then the purposes of the hospice idea—namely, that the patient should be surrounded by his dear ones during his last days, and that he should not be surrounded and subjected to useless medical apparatus and practice—all this is fully in accord with Jewish tradition.

It might be added that since part of the work with the dying patients in the hospice may involve the transmission of religious ideas which are consoling, there is a great deal in Jewish tradition which would well be usable for this purpose. Just to mention three instances: Job (3:13), speaking of death, refers to it as a quiet sleep. He says, "For now [i.e., had I died] I would have lain still and been quiet; I should have slept and then had been at rest." In fact, even more than the idea that death is peace and rest is the thought ascribed to Rabbi Meir *(Genesis Rabba* 9:5) that death is one of God's most blessed creations. He refers to the fact that God, having performed the work of Creation, commented and said, "It is very good." Rabbi Meir said that among the things that God considered very good, i.e., a boon to mankind, in His Creation, was also the blessing of death.

Also, because Scripture says of Moses and Aaron that they died by the Mouth of God (Numbers 33:38, Deuteronomy 34:5) i.e., the Word of God, the Talmud *(Berachos* 8a) takes this to mean that they died with God's Kiss. Since then, every peaceful, quiet death is described as *mayss b'n'shika,* "death by the Kiss of God."

17

QUESTIONS CONCERNING PROSELYTES

(1) Is it required by the Halachah to give a proselyte a new and a Jewish name, such as Abraham for men and Ruth for women, for example? (2) Is the acquiring of proselytes a *mitzvah*? In other words, is it our duty to seek and search for proselytes? (3) Which commandments have to be explained to the proselyte before he is accepted? (Asked by Rabbi Allen S. Maller, Culver City, California.)

ANSWER:

THERE SEEMS to be no statement anywhere in the law requiring that the proselyte be given a new and a Jewish name. The laws covering proselytism are given in great detail, and if there were any such requirements, it would certainly be mentioned. Nevertheless, in spite of the law not seeming to require it, the giving of a Jewish name must have been a fairly widespread custom. There is the proselyte named Obadiah to whom Maimonides addressed his famous letter. It is highly unlikely that a Christian at baptism would have been given the name of one of the minor Hebrew prophets. This, then, was his new name. Also the *Tosfos* quotes (with respect) the opinion of "Abraham the proselyte" (*Kiddushin* 71b). So renaming the proselytes was not required but was frequently practiced.

The second question seems to be implied in the many Talmudic discussions on proselytes. There are opinions, for example, strongly opposed to accepting proselytes. In *Yevamos* 109b, Rabbi Isaac says, "Evil after evil comes from those who accept proselytes," but the Talmud immediately explains away this negative opinion and says that evil comes from those who try to urge and persuade people to become proselytes. But if we do not try to persuade them and they come of their own free will, then it is a *mitzvah* to accept them, especially if we are convinced that their motives are worthy. The proof that it was not a mandate to go forth and seek proselytes is the fact that they never accepted proselytes in the days of David and Solomon because the proselytes would be lured by the grandeur of the Jewish kingdom and therefore their motives would not be pure. In other words, we should welcome proselytes. That is a *mitzvah,* but to go and persuade them to come to us seems to be considered improper. All the various opinions on this question are well summarized in the *Encyclopedia Talmudit,* in the second article on the question (*"Gerut,"* at the beginning of the article). The answer, therefore, can be put this way: It is a *mitzvah* to *accept* a worthy proselyte, but not to engage in missionary activity, searching for proselytes.

Regarding the third question, the Talmud (in *Yevamos* 47a) and the *Shulchan Aruch* (in *Yore Deah* 268:1) put the answer as follows: We teach them *some (miktsas)* of the lighter commandments *(kalos)* and some of the stricter commandments *(chamuros)*. But the sources do not give too many details. The *Shulchan Aruch* says, also, we teach them the essentials of the law *(ikre ha-das)*. The various sources mention certain laws, we might say, sporadically. For example, the men are told about leaving the corner of the field for the poor *(Yevamos* 47b); otherwise, they might kill an indigent gleaner, thinking him a robber. Others mention that the women are taught their three chief commandments as to menses, *challa,* and kindling of the lights, but in general the law states that we do not go into the matters in detail *(en marbin olov, Yevamos* 47b).

18

AN INCOMPLETE CONVERSION

QUESTION:

A Gentile girl married a Jewish man. Immediately after the marriage, she began the process of conversion before a Reform rabbi. She took the course of instruction in a proselyte class conducted by the rabbi. However, she did not participate in the final ceremony of conversion because she became pregnant. After two children were born to her, she returned to participate in the final ceremony of conversion, and she and her family have been living a Jewish life. But since her children were born before the final ceremony of conversion, she is now greatly concerned whether her children are Jewish or not. What is the status of her children? (Asked by L.S.F.)

ANSWER:

IF THE PROCESS of conversion had been carried out according to Orthodox law, it would seem evident that the children are not Jewish by birth since their mother was not completely converted when she gave birth to them. However, in Orthodox law, there is a strong tendency to protect the Jewish status of children. Thus, if a man comes and says that he had been converted in some other city, he is not believed until he brings proof. His conversion is in doubt, but he is not permitted to cast doubt on the

Jewishness of his children (*Yore Deah* 268:11). Also,
while the ceremonies of circumcision for a man and the
mikvah for a woman and a man are, of course, essential in
the Orthodox procedure, nevertheless, there is considerable indication that these final ceremonies are not the most
important. There are two elements in the conversion
process which are the most heavily stressed, one, the
understanding and the acceptance of the commandments,
and two, retrospectively, the life which has been led by the
proselyte after the conversion or the claimed conversion.

The special stress placed on learning and accepting the
commandments can be seen from the fact that the ceremonial bathing may be considered valid if it is not done in the
presence of three, but the study and the acceptance of the
commandments must be in the presence of three (prefera-
bly learned) men. Special stress is put not only upon the
commandments, but also upon the Jewishness of the life
led by the convert or by one who claims he is a convert. If a
Gentile claims to have been converted in some other city,
he must bring proof of the fact, but if he is seen to be living
a Jewish life, observing the commandments, he is to be
considered a true proselyte (*Yore Deah* 268:10). So, too,
in the case of a minor who is converted—he may repudiate
the conversion when he grows up, but if he has been living
a Jewish life, that fact is decisive and his conversion is
permanent. As for the importance of the conversion
mikvah, even that is diminished by the following: If a man
or a woman takes a ritual bath for some other purpose than
conversion, this bath may be accepted as valid for conversion, although that was not the original intention (*Yore
Deah* 268:3).

Yet, although the greater emphasis in the entire conversion process is on the spiritual and ethical elements, it would, of course, be incorrect to say that the purely ceremonial procedures, being secondary, may be set aside. Even though Rabbi Eliezer doubts the necessity of the ritual bath and says that a man is a full proselyte if he does not take the ritual bath but is circumcised, and even though Rabbi Joshua deprecates the necessity of circumcision and says that a man is a full proselyte if he is bathed but not circumcised (*Yevamos* 46a), actually both ceremonies are required. Therefore in the case of this woman, even though she took the instruction and even though she kept a Jewish home, she would not be considered a proselyte, and her two children, therefore, would not be Jewish.

It must be added that although the child was conceived while she was still a Gentile, yet if she had continued in the conversion process and the child had been born after her conversion was complete, then the child would be Jewish. This would be true even if the father was a Gentile, for the child that she was carrying would be deemed to have been converted with her (see *Modern Reform Responsa,* pp. 143 ff., and *Yore Deah* 268:6).

But all the above is theoretical in the case which we are discussing, since the conversion process was under the guidance of a Reform rabbi. Reform Judaism has made a drastic change in the conversion process. One might say that the stress placed on the intellectual and spiritual elements in the Orthodox conversion Halachah became decisive in the development of the Reform ritual. The two purely ceremonial rituals, circumcision and *mikvah,* are disregarded. They are no longer required. But the intellectual and ethical elements are strengthened. The Reform process of conversion involves a much longer and more complete course of training than the Orthodox practice requires. As for the closing ceremony after the instruction (in Orthodoxy this means circumcision and/or *mikvah*), in Reform it is not much more than a sort of solemn commencement exercise, a giving of a certificate after the study course is completed.

Since, therefore, the woman took the instruction, which is the important part of the Reform conversion process, and since she considers herself Jewish and her home Jewish, her conversion in this case may well be considered complete, for the sake of her children, even if she did not participate in the formal closing ceremony until after the children were born. Her children, therefore, from the point of view of Reform are fully Jewish. Even if they were to be deemed not Jewish, which in this case would be contrary to the spirit of Reform Judaism, the CCAR has decided that such children, if given full instruction in our religious schools, need no further acts of ritual conversion.

19

OWNERSHIP OF THE BODY OF THE DEAD

QUESTION:

The events dealt with in this inquiry occurred a full generation ago. A prominent member of our temple was married to
an unconverted Christian woman. He died, and in his will he
had specified that he be buried in the lot that he owned in our
congregational cemetery. His widow, however, wanted him
to be buried in her Christian cemetery. Eugene B. Strassburger, the executor of the will, put the question to a group
of judges, and they decided that the deceased has no ownership of his body and that his heir (in this case, his widow)
has the full right to dispose of the body as she wishes. Thus
the body of this man was buried in the Christian cemetery.
Since such a situation may recur, the question is now asked:
What is Jewish law on this matter? Who owns and has the
right of disposal of a person's body? (Asked by Eugene B.
Strassburger, Pittsburgh, Pennsylvania.)

ANSWER:

ON THE FACE of it, at least from the point of view of Jewish
law, the decision of the judges seems inconsistent. The
American law agrees that the deceased, through his last
will and testament, continues to control the disposal of his
property and yet has lost all control over his own body.
This would mean, also, for example, that if the deceased
had provided in his will that his body be buried, and his
widow preferred to have his body cremated, her decision

would stand against that of the deceased. The question, therefore, is rather an important one, namely, what is the attitude of Jewish law on the general question of the right of deciding on the disposal of the body, as, for example, whether it should be buried in one city or another? In brief, who, according to Jewish law, has the ownership of the body of the deceased?

It must be understood at the outset that there is a basic difference between any canon law and secular law. Canon law, being religious, is guided by the presuppositions of religion which underlie its legal enactments. Jewish law is canon law—religious law—and therefore, underlying all discussion of the legal question involved, there are certain basic religious presuppositions. Primarily, these presuppositions can be summed up in the religious (in this case, the Jewish) concept of the human personality. A human being is more than a body. He is also a spirit, a soul, which survives after the death of the body. Therefore the person continues to be a person and to have certain personal rights even after the body dies. In Jewish lore, the man's spirit not only persists after death (as most religions maintain) but is also believed to hover about the body for some time after death. This concept tends to give the body more than the status of a piece of clay. A number of examples will indicate how this religious belief leads to the further belief that even after death, and certainly immediately after death, the body and its accompanying spirit remain a person with certain human rights. A number of regulations are based upon this general idea. For example, it is forbidden in the presence of the dead to speak of anything except matters that concern the dead, namely, the burial, the mourning, the tombstone, etc. (*Yore Deah* 344:10). No idle, irrelevant chatter is permitted in the presence of the dead. Another example is the prohibition of going into a cemetery wearing phylacteries *(tefillin)* or carrying a scroll of the law (Torah) because the dead no longer have the privilege of observing these rituals and are presumed to be sad at not being able to have the privilege of obeying these commandments *(Yore Deah* 367:3). This sin of carrying a Torah, etc., into the cemetery, which presumably would sadden the departed, is called the sin of "mocking the poor," a description based upon the verse in Proverbs 17:5: "He who mocks the poor blasphemes his Creator." The dead are no longer in duty bound to obey the commandments *(Shabbat* 30a), and it is presumed that they are sad at that deprivation. Furthermore, it is deemed preferable to hold the seven-day mourning period *(shiva)* with the accompanying public prayers in the home where the person had lived at the time of his death. This is because of the belief that the spirit, sad at leaving this life, still hovers for a while around the home, and that the public prayers offered there bring him consolation *(Chochmas Adam* 165:11). In less mystic terms, we might say that the awareness of the presence of the departed is strongest in the home in which he has lived.

All these rather mystical concepts add up to the same attitude held with regard to the recently departed, namely, that the departed is more than lifeless clay but constitutes, to some extent, a personality that must be respected and that still has certain rights. These beliefs, which to some extent may be considered folkloristic, are, nevertheless, revelatory of a basic attitude of the dead as a continuing personality.

Such a basic attitude naturally is carried over into

questions of practical law, as is the question which is asked
here. One practical question is the following: If the
departed is to be considered to some extent still a person, is
this shadowy person able to acquire property? On this
question, the great legalist Maimonides says flatly that the
dead cannot acquire property *(eyn kinyon l'mays) (Yad,
Hil. Matana* 10:12). However, this outright denial by
Maimonides of the possibility of the dead acquiring
property is controverted by other authorities. See the great
Spanish scholar Solomon ben Aderet (12th century), in his
Responsa #375, who discusses the following question: A
man turned over a sum of money to an agent to be used for
tombstones, etc., for a certain deceased. Money turned
over to an agent is deemed to have been formally acquired
by the person represented by the agent. But the donor
changed his mind and wanted the money back from the
agent, arguing that since the dead cannot acquire property,
the money was still rightfully his and he could take it back.
But the agent argued on the other side of the question, as
follows: The Mishnah says *(Shekalim* 2:5) that if money is
collected among friends for the dead, grave, tombstone,
etc., and some money is left over, the leftover money goes
to the dead man's heirs. Clearly, then, if the dead man's
heirs may have the rest of the collected money, the dead
man has indeed acquired it and has bequeathed the rest of
it. Solomon ben Aderet agrees with this reasoning, and so
he would hold that the dead can indeed acquire property.

Another, more telling example is the following: If the
body of a slain man is found buried in a field, and the body
must be removed to be buried in a cemetery, the body
cannot be taken by itself, but a certain amount of earth

must be taken with it on the principle clearly stated in the law that the dead *acquires* the place where he is put or found (*Sanhedrin* 47b and *Yore Deah* 364:3).

Among the other legal rights of the dead, besides the possibility of acquiring money or land, is the right to determine where he shall be buried. This right goes back to the earliest possible source, namely, the Torah. In Genesis 47:29–30, Jacob in Egypt calls his son Joseph and says, "When I die, do not bury me in Egypt, but take my body and bury it with my ancestors in the land of Canaan." This wish was, of course, obeyed, and such a wish is always obeyed, as is indicated in another case cited and dealt with by the great Spanish Jewish authority cited above, Solomon ben Aderet (responsum #369 and cited by Isserles, *Yore Deah* 363:2). The case was as follows: A man and his sons were away from home in another city. The man was dying, and he told his sons that when he died he wanted to be buried in their home-city, where their ancestors were buried. But when he died it was impossible to carry out his wish (the roads became unsafe, perhaps because of war), and he was buried in the city in which they were temporarily. Some months later the roads had become safe again, and it became possible to transport the body. But the body by now had so decayed that it was impossible to move it (they did not use complete coffins). Thereupon Solomon ben Aderet permitted the family to put quicklime over the body to complete the decay of the flesh so that the bones could be transported and the father's wish be carried out. Now if so drastic a step as putting quicklime on the body was permitted by a great authority for the purpose of carrying out the deceased's desire as to where he should be

buried, then it is evident how strongly founded in Jewish
law is the right of the deceased to determine his resting-
place.

To sum up: In Jewish law, which is a religious law, the
deceased retains some personality, especially near the time
following death. Therefore the deceased has certain rights
of a person—the right to be respected and even, according
to some authorities, the right to acquire property. But
without question the deceased has the right to determine
where his body shall be buried. Of course, this right of the
departed to determine the disposal of his body is not an
absolute right. It is limited by other requirements of Jewish
law. A man has no right to demand that his body be
handled in a way that is violative of Jewish law. Jewish law
is opposed to cremation. It requires burial. If a man says,
"Do not bury my body," his request is not to be heeded
since this request is contrary to Jewish law (*Shulchan
Aruch, Yore Deah* 348:3). But of course, as to *where* his
body should be buried, his right of decision cannot be
controverted.

20

A FORMER CHRISTIAN CEMETERY

QUESTION:

A Methodist church intends to sell its present cemetery. It will remove the bodies buried there and rebury them in another church cemetery. May a Jewish congregation buy the vacated acreage for use as a Jewish cemetery? (Asked by Rabbi Richard J. Sobel, Succasunna, New Jersey.)

ANSWER:

IT IS AN established custom for Jewish congregations to have their own local cemetery in order to obviate the necessity of transferring the dead from one city to another (see the responsa of Isaac Spektor, *Eyn Yitzchok, Yore Deah #34*, and Greenwald, *Kol Bo,* p. 162). Even if it is necessary by municipal ordinance to participate in a joint cemetery, the Jewish community must have a separate Jewish section in which it will have complete control over the burials. Therefore the intention of this congregation to buy a cemetery of its own is to be looked upon as a laudatory *mitzvah* which might outweigh many possible objections. But what objection *can* there be to the fulfillment of this *mitzvah* by the purchase of land which had been vacated as a Christian cemetery?

First of all, it should be stated that a Christian cemetery,

even with all the Christian graves in it, is looked upon in
Jewish law with respectful sanctity. The Talmud in *Taanis*
16a discusses the custom of going to the cemetery to pray
during fast-days. The question is asked there what the
purpose is of going on fast-days to pray in the cemetery.
The Talmud gives two possible answers. We go in order
that the dead may pray in our behalf. For that purpose we
go to a Jewish cemetery to pray. Or it may also be that we
go in order to be humbled before God in the presence of the
dead, and for that purpose we may go also to non-Jewish
cemeteries to pray.

But the question arises whether there is any objection in
Jewish law to the reuse of graves in which other bodies had
formerly been buried. Leaving aside the question of
Jewish or Christian graves, there are certain rules which
may remain in people's minds as vague objections. The
Shulchan Aruch (Yore Deah 364:6) says that a grave that is
dug for the burial of one's father or mother and is not used
for that purpose may not be used by anybody else. But this,
the *Shulchan Aruch* explains, is a special honor to the
memory of one's own parents. It therefore does not apply
to other graves and other burials. It is a special case.

There is also a further restriction to the reuse of graves.
The *Shulchan Aruch (Yore Deah* 364:1) says that a *built-up*
grave *(kever binyon)* used for one body, or even intended
for one body, may not be used for any other body. This
refers to a sort of a private mausoleum or structure built
over a grave. But the *Shulchan Aruch* continues that the
earth of the grave *(karka olom)* cannot be forbidden for
reuse. Besides, we may assume in this specific case that
after the Methodist church removes the bodies, it is not

likely to leave the ground with all the former graves open, but will undoubtedly run a bulldozer over the acreage to level the ground off. In any case, as the *Shulchan Aruch* says clearly, only an erected grave can be forbidden, but not the ground itself.

As a matter of relevant historical fact, there is a record of a Jewish congregation that bought back a cemetery that was used as a Christian cemetery. Greenwald *(Kol Bo Al Avelus,* p. 168, note 9) refers to the responsa of Jacob Weil (#94), who tells of the congregation in Wuerzberg, whose cemetery had been confiscated by the ruler when he expelled the Jews from the city. He sold the cemetery to Gentiles (presumably to be used by them as a cemetery). When the Jews were permitted to return to Wuerzberg, they wanted to buy the cemetery back. The specific question asked of Jacob Weil was whether they might cut down the trees and sell the lumber to raise funds to buy back the cemetery. They naturally wanted to buy back their old cemetery, and there is no record that they felt any ground for hesitation because during their exile it was used as a Christian cemetery.

To sum up: The *mitzvah* of owning a cemetery should outweigh any minor objection. Even a Christian cemetery as such has a respectful sanctity in Jewish law. The prohibition against reuse of graves applies specifically to graves dug for one's parents and also to built-up mausoleum-type graves. The earth itself is not prohibited. Finally, there is a record of a historic congregation willing to buy a cemetery even though it was presumably used as a Christian cemetery.

21

GENTILES BURIED IN A JEWISH CEMETERY

QUESTION:

The cemetery of a small Jewish community is actually a section of a large general cemetery. Through some error, possibly, some Gentiles were buried in the Jewish section. Certain pious members of the community are indignant at this fact and wonder what to do. What is the Halachic status of this situation? (Asked by Louis J. Freehof, San Francisco.)

ANSWER:

THE SPECIFICALLY Jewish cemetery does not have a firm status in Jewish law, as does, for example, the synagogue. However, it has become an established tradition to have a separate Jewish cemetery. In the days of the Mishnah, there were family cemeteries but not communal cemeteries. The later-developed tradition of a separate Jewish communal cemetery also had the form of a Jewish section in a general cemetery (see *Reform Responsa,* p. 161). And when such exist, here and in Europe, it is clearly understood that only Jews may be buried in the Jewish section. But what is to be done under the special circumstances in the question asked, when for some reason, Gentile bodies were placed in the Jewish section? Does this fact affect in any way the sanctity of the Jewish cemetery?

The answer to this question cannot be given precisely because, as far as I can recall, there is no reference to such an occurrence in the past legal literature. So the question of the effect of the presence of the Gentile bodies must be decided by analogy with past recorded attitudes to the law.

First, it must be understood that the Jewish law has a definite reverence and even a religious obligation to the bodies of non-Jews. The law as stated in *Gittin* is that we are in duty bound to visit the sick of Gentiles, to bury their dead, and to comfort their mourners. To which, however, Rashi says: to bury their dead but not in the Jewish cemetery (he says this even though the law distinctly says, "We bury their dead *with* the Jewish dead"). So Gentiles may not be buried in the Jewish cemetery, but we do have a Jewish duty to give them burial if needed.

Now, what is the effect of the presence of these bodies in our cemetery? Do they inhibit our own religious functions? The answer to this is definitely no. The Talmud in *Taanis* says that one of the ways of humbling ourselves during fast-days is to visit the cemetery. If there are no Jewish cemeteries available, we may visit on fast-days the Gentile cemeteries, so as to feel humble in the presence of the dead. So it is clear that although the dead are all Gentile, as in a Gentile cemetery, the Talmud does not consider that their presence hinders but, on the contrary, helps a religious purpose.

Now there is a third and negative point to consider: the question of good and ill will. If the Jewish community in this small town insisted that the presence of the Gentile bodies is intolerable (which it really is not), and if the community insisted on having the bodies removed as an unbearable intrusion in the Jewish cemetery, it would certainly create ill will and harm the Jewish community. Much is permitted in Jewish law to avoid ill will. An analogy is not irrelevant here: A *mezuzah* is required only in a house inhabited by a Jew. If a Jew moves out of a house and a Gentile will then occupy the house, the *mezuzah* must be removed. However, says the great authority Moses Isserles, if removing the *mezuzah* will create ill will, it may be allowed to remain in this house occupied by a Gentile.

In the light of the above, what should the Jewish community do? It is an established Jewish custom that no Gentiles be buried in a Jewish cemetery. This incident gives the Jewish community the right to insist on guarantees that this shall not occur again. If family or communal situations are such that the reburial of these bodies in a Gentile section will not create ill will, that should be done. If that cannot be done, then if it will not create ill will, the bodies can be moved and buried near the fence, as is done in some traditions with Jewish suicides. If that cannot be done either, without creating ill will, then they should be left where they are. The body of a Gentile involves obligation and a certain sanctity in Jewish law. Its presence does not inhibit the mood of sanctity. Therefore, use this occasion for reassertion of the right of exclusive burial, move the bodies if it will not create ill will to do so, otherwise let them remain. The cemetery remains Jewish and sacred.

Added note: There is considerable discussion in the law as to who may be buried beside whom, the righteous besides the wicked, a man beside a woman not his wife. If the Gentile bodies referred to are buried in the row of graves, i.e., not in a separate family group, some pious people may object to burial alongside. Therefore it might be practical to leave the space of one grave between.

22

AGED PARENT TO NURSING HOME

QUESTION:

If an aged parent who now lives with his family is feeble to such an extent that he would be much better cared for in a nursing home, but if he strenuously objects to leaving the family home, what in the light of Jewish tradition can be done under these circumstances? (Asked by Rabbi Marc Saperstein, Canton, Massachusetts.)

ANSWER:

THERE IS a great deal of writing, opinion, and law in Jewish tradition as to the duties of children to a parent. The original source of all the legislation on the subject is toward the end of Chapter 1 of Talmud *Kiddushin* (31a ff.), where the reciprocal duties of parents' obligations to children and children's obligations to parents are discussed in great detail. These Talmudic discussions were continued through the centuries and are now crystallized in a complete section in the *Shulchan Aruch, Yore Deah* 240 and 241, under the heading, "The Laws of Honoring Father and Mother."

These laws deal with the duty of respecting the dignity of the parent, of sustaining him and providing for him, and even of enduring the unreasonableness of a parent. See, for example, 240:8: "How far must the respect for parents go?

Even if the parent took the son's purse of gold coins and cast it into the sea, the son must not shame the parent or lose his temper in his presence, but must accept the Scriptural mandate [of respect] and remain silent.'' One must not even annoy a parent. The Talmud (31a) says: ''God says if a man vexes his parent, God does not dwell in that house because, He says, 'If I dwelt there among them, they would vex Me too.' '' These are cited as exemplifications of considerable detailed law of how the commandment of honoring parents was carried out to a most reverent extreme.

All of this is, of course, well known. But these laws become especially difficult to follow in modern times. In earlier years, there was no place for a parent who was failing in health to be taken care of except in the family home, but nowadays the situation has changed. Now there are homes for the aged with hospital facilities, and there are nursing homes devoted especially to the care of the aged. If these institutions are well conducted by responsible people, there is no question that the old person can be taken care of (at least from the physical point of view) much better than he could be taken care of at home. But the difficulty is psychological or emotional. Often, or even most of the time, the parent does not wish to leave the home of his dear ones and become a stranger among strangers, and his or her unwillingness to go must be counted as at least one element in the parent's welfare. If the parent finally consents against his or her will and leaves the house in bitter resentment, there can be estrangement in the family and even the loss of the will to recover health on the part of the parent. So, basically, this situation, when

it arises, is a hopeless one, and there can be no easy
solution.

Does Jewish tradition give us at least a modicum of
guidance in this matter? In this regard there is a discussion
which is given most fully in the Yerushalmi (also toward
the end of the first chapter of tractate *Kiddushin;* it is found
more briefly in our Babylonian Talmud at the bottom of
page 31a). The statement is as follows: "It may happen
that a son will feed his father the finest of food and yet the
son deserves the punishment of hell. On the other hand, it
may be that the son will bind his father to the millstone to
grind grain and yet that son will deserve the blessing of
Paradise. How can this be? In the first case, the father asks
the son, 'Where did you get all these dainties, my son?'
and the son answers gruffly, 'Eat and be silent like a dog
eats.' In the other case, the heathen king had summoned all
owners of grist mills to be captured into permanent
slavery, and the son says to the father (who still owns the
mill), 'Father, I will say that I am the owner and will go
and be enslaved in your place, while you will pretend to be
a mere employee who is hired to grind the grain.' This son
who forces his father to a miserable task in order to save
him from a worse misery deserves Paradise."

Evidently this supposed case was not looked upon as a
mere hypothetical situation, but was considered to be
expressive of an important line of action, for not only is it
found in both Talmuds, but it is embodied, one might say,
as law in the *Shulchan Aruch, Yore Deah* 240:4, Isserles.
He says, "If the son makes the father grind at the millstone
but his intention is for the benefit of the father, to save him
from a worse situation, then the son should talk gently to

the father and convince the father that his intention is for the father's benefit, until the father finally consents to grind at the millstone. This son will inherit Paradise.''

The implication of this narrative embodied in the law is clear enough. It will often happen that the idea of leaving home and going to a nursing home is as bitter a prospect to the father as grinding at the millstone, but if it is not merely to relieve the children of the burden of his care, but is really for the benefit of the father, then it is the duty of the son or daughter to try, as Isserles says, to allay the objections and to persuade the parent until he consents.

In other words, whatever guidance this gives us is as follows: First the children must be sure of their motives. If they are sure that their motives are not selfish, but for the good of the parent, then it is their duty to reason with him until he consents, if only reluctantly. To insist that he leave the home over his strenuous objection, would be wrong. It is their duty, as Isserles says, "to speak words of kindness to the heart of the father and to show the father that his intention is for his own good,'' and to keep up this gentle persuasion until the father consents.

Addendum

As a matter of fact, the legal literature does contain something analogous to the modern practice of sending a parent to an institution such as an old folks' home. Maimonides (*Hil. Mamrim* 6:10, based upon the Talmudic incident of Rabbi Assi, *Kiddushin* 31b), says that if a parent has become insane and it is impossible for the child to take care of him, he may leave him to the care of others.

The *Rabed* to that passage disagrees with Maimonides, but Joseph Caro defends Maimonides in his *Bes Joseph* to the *Tur* (*Yore Deah* 240) and embodies this as a law in his own *Shulchan Aruch* (*Yore Deah* 240:10).

23

AN UNFILLED GRAVE

QUESTION:

A funeral took place late in the afternoon toward evening. The gravediggers' union forbids its members to work after a certain hour. The coffin was put in the grave, and before the grave was filled, the gravediggers stopped work. This raised the following question: Does the period of mourning begin, even though the grave was not filled and the burial thus not completed? (Asked by Louis J. Freehof, San Francisco, California.)

ANSWER:

UNTIL THE BURIAL is completed, the mourners are not yet technically *avelim,* who are in duty bound to begin their mourning of seven days, of thirty days, etc. Until the burial, they are still *onaynim.* An *onayn* may not participate in any *mitzvos* (even prayers) because the duty of burial for the *onayn* takes precedent over all other commandments. So the question in the law is: When is the burial considered to be completed so that the bereaved ceases to be an *onayn* and becomes an *ovel,* who must now fulfill the duty of mourning, *shiva, shloshim,* etc.? In other words, what constitutes the complete burial?

On this question there is a classic dispute between two

97

great authorities, Rashi and his grandson, Rabbenu Tam. The dispute is first described in the *Tosfos* to *Kesuvos* 4b and is discussed by the *Tur* (*Yore Deah* 375) and the *Taz* to the *Shulchan Aruch* (same reference). The dispute between the two authorities centers around the phrase used by Rabbi Joshua in *Moed Katan* 27a. He says that the mourning begins (i.e., the *onayn* becomes an *ovel*) when the *gollel* is closed. The basis of the disagreement is as to the meaning of the word *gollel*. It means something round that can be rolled. When they buried in caves, as they did in Palestine at the time of the Mishnah, after the body was put into the niche within the cave, they rolled a huge stone which closed the entrance to the cave. (By the way, this can be noted in the description of the grave in which Jesus was buried. The sentence used there is, "The angel of the Lord descended from heaven and came and rolled back the stone from the door [of the sepulcher]" [Matthew 28:2].)

But the problem of the meaning of *gollel* arose when the practice of burial in caves stopped and people were buried in graves in the earth. What meaning could now be given to the phrase of Rabbi Joshua that mourning begins when the *gollel* (the round stone) seals the cave or the grave?

Rashi's opinion is that sealing the *gollel* now means that once the coffin is closed and is ready for burial, the man is an *ovel* and the mourning can begin. In this opinion, he is supported by Nachmanides. However, his grandson Rabbenu Tam said that the sealing of the *gollel* means the complete filling up of the grave.

Most authorities agree with Rabbenu Tam, and so the *Tur* quotes his father, the *Rosh,* to that effect, and so Joseph Caro, in the *Shulchan Aruch* (*Yore Deah* 371), says that the mourning begins only when the grave is filled with earth. This is now the general practice, and mourning does not begin until the grave is filled.

However, the opinion of Rashi that the closing of the *gollel* means the sealing of the coffin, and that mourning can begin when the coffin is sealed, still has weight under special circumstances. So, for example, the law is clear (*Shulchan Aruch, Yore Deah* 375:2) that when the burial takes place in a different city, the mourners staying in the first city begin their mourning when they see the coffin leaving the city. So in a sense they are following Rashi's opinion under these special circumstances. So, also, for example, in an emergency such as a gravediggers' strike, when bodies cannot be buried perhaps for weeks, we rely on Rashi's opinion and begin the mourning once the coffin is sealed and put away.

To sum up: By general law and custom, mourning should not begin until the grave is filled, but in emergencies such as this, when the union rules forbid the filling of the grave at this late hour, it can be considered an emergency and we rely on Rashi's opinion and begin the mourning at once. Of course, it would be much more preferable if the funeral were held earlier because, anyhow, there is objection to burial at night (cf. Greenwald, *Kol Bo,* p. 188, par. 24).

24

FREEZING A BODY FOR LATER FUNERAL

QUESTION:

A member of the congregation desires to make arrangements
for his body to be frozen after his death (by an institution in
California which does this work). The purpose of this
procedure is so that he can be buried in one funeral service
with his wife when she dies. What would be the attitude of
the Halachah to this plan? (Asked by Rabbi Norman M.
Goldburg, Augusta, Georgia.)

ANSWER:

THE INTENTION described in the letter is a very curious
one. As far as I know, the question has never been asked
before, but then the technique of freezing bodies
(cryobiology) was not known until recently. In the past and
all through our tradition, desire has been expressed for
families to be buried in the same *place*. This request has
considerable attention and approbation in Jewish law,
especially when the burial is to be in a *family* plot *(kever
ovos)*, but this is the first time I have heard of a desire and a
plan which goes beyond the husband and wife being buried
in one place, but is a plan to have them buried at the same
time. The request is indeed a strange one, for, after all,
how can one know (unless one is already in a dying
condition) just when he will die? Perhaps his wife will die

first. Will he, then, make arrangements for her body to be frozen? Has she consented to that? Or suppose she marries again. But this latter contingency has not much bearing on the problem because if a twice-married woman dies, the custom is that she is buried with the husband with whom she has had children.

Now the question is whether this wish to be frozen for later burial is in agreement with Jewish legal tradition. There is a discussion on the freezing of bodies in *Current Reform Responsa,* pp. 238 ff. but that discussion has to do with the freezing of the body of a person still alive. The theory behind that was that the person would be kept in suspended animation by freezing until some future time when medical science would discover a cure for the disease from which he suffers, and which at the present time is deemed incurable. But the question here involves the freezing of a dead body. The first question, then, is whether there is any analogy to such a procedure in the tradition. In a way there is. One might say that the *purpose* of the proposed freezing of the body is the same as that of the embalming practiced originally by the ancient Egyptians (and done to the bodies of Jacob and Joseph) and, also, of the embalming widely practiced in modern times, namely, to delay the decomposition of the body.

Is the process of embalming, to which this new freezing is analogous in purpose, to be considered acceptable in Jewish law? According to some authorities, something much like it was actually practiced in the past and is to some extent permissible today. Greenwald (in his *Kol Bo,* p. 61) objects to the *usual* type of embalming, which involves cutting up the body and removing some of the internal organs. This procedure constitutes mutilation of the dead *(nivvul ha-mayss),* which is forbidden by Jewish law. However, Greenwald then speaks of a modern embalming process which involves no cutting into the body but is done merely by injection. This type of embalming he actually calls "freezing." Then he proceeds to give authorities who make this "freezing" acceptable. One is particularly interesting to us—Kimchi to I Samuel 31:12, which speaks of the men of Beth-shan, of whom Scripture says that they *burned* the bodies of Saul and Jonathan, which had been mutilated by the Philistines. The commentator Kimchi says that whenever burning of bodies is mentioned in Scripture, it does not mean actually burning, but something like embalming. Greenwald also refers to a modern authority, Baumol, who in his responsa *(Emek Halacha,* #48 and #49) accepts the type of embalming called "freezing." From all this, we can say that this method of preserving the body from decomposition, if there is a good reason for the delay, is not in itself unacceptable in Jewish law, provided that the preserving of the body is not done in a way that mutilates the body; and the cryobiology method certainly does not mutilate the body.

However, even though there are no strong objections to the method of preserving the body, there are objections to the *delay* in burial of a body. Jewish law and custom require that burial take place as soon as possible after the death; in fact, according to Orthodox practice, if it is possible, burial is on the same day. Only after the body is buried can the formal process of mourning begin *(shiva, shloshim,* etc.). In this case, if the body will not be buried for months or years, when is the required mourning to take place? Mourning is an honor and a piety to which every child of Israel is entitled. Besides the honor due the dead, it is a *mitzvah* incumbent on the survivors to give the dead due mourning. This plan, by not allowing the body to be buried, is preventing his family from fulfilling an important *mitzvah,* which one has no right to do.

There is also another objection to the delay in burial. Tradition declares that the period of death and the decay of the body is the time when all sins are forgiven. This is based upon the account of the criminals in Mishnah *Sanhedrin* 6:6, where we are told that the criminals were first buried in the cemetery belonging to the court. Only after their flesh had decayed could their families take the bones to bury them in the family cemetery, because once the flesh is gone, all the sins are forgiven. Therefore, even if, as mentioned above, the type of embalming called "freezing" is not objectionable, the preserving of the body for a long time, and thus keeping it from normal decomposition, *is* objectionable. It is for this reason that older Jewish tradition wanted the body to be directly in contact with earth and used, therefore, loose boards instead of a complete coffin—all this to *hasten* decomposition. But today we compromise in Orthodox custom by putting a little earth on the body inside the coffin. (As to contact with earth to hasten decomposition, see *Yore Deah* 362:1 and especially the *Be'er Hetev*.)

All of this indicates a general objection, if not a clear-cut prohibition, on the part of tradition to the procedure asked about here. It delays the burial, keeping the survivors from the *mitzvah* of mourning. It delays the funeral, which in itself is objectionable, and hinders the normal decomposition of the body, which is deemed in tradition to be a signal for the complete forgiveness of sin.

However, the desire on the part of the inquirer to be buried at the same time as his wife, while it is unusual, is not an unworthy sentiment. Perhaps it can be carried out in some other way which does not involve all the objections mentioned above. Let the man, when he dies, be buried in a single grave and not in his family plot. Then, when his wife dies, his body can be disinterred to be buried with her in the family plot. Burial in the family plot is one of the reasons why disinterment is permitted in Jewish law (*Yore Deah* 363:1). Then, at the time of the disinterment, a double funeral service can be conducted or, at least, the funeral address can make adequate reference to both of the departed. There is no objection in the law either to the disinterment or to the delayed funeral service *(hesped)*. In this way the families will not be deprived of the duty of mourning, the body will be buried in proper time, and the desire of the inquirer can be fulfilled in full accordance with tradition.

25

BURIAL IN A NATIONAL CEMETERY

QUESTION:

A Jewish veteran has asked whether it is permissible, from
the point of view of Jewish tradition, for him to be buried in
the national cemetery instead of in a Jewish cemetery.
(Asked by Rabbi Bennett M. Hermann, East Meadow, New
York.)

ANSWER:

DURING WARTIME the Jewish Chaplaincy Commission,
composed of Orthodox, Conservative, and Reform rabbis,
was confronted with the problem of whether or not it is
permissible for a Jewish soldier to be buried at Arlington or
any other national cemetery. The question arose because
of a proposal made at that time to establish other national
cemeteries in addition to Arlington; and so there would be
plenty of space for the bodies of such veterans who had the
right to be buried in a national cemetery.

The situation before the committee was not quite the
same as the earlier situation with regard to Jewish soldiers
fallen in battle. During and after wartime, cemeteries were
established near the chief battlefields in Europe, and many
Jewish soldiers fallen in battle were buried there. There is
no objection at all, from the point of view of Jewish law,
for a Jewish soldier who has fallen in battle to be buried

where he fell (or near there), because a fallen soldier is considered a *mayss mitzvah,* i.e., a body which we are in duty bound to bury, who, according to the law, acquires possession of the place where he has fallen. Thus, according to the law, if a body is found in someone else's field, he may be buried there, for a *mayss mitzvah* acquires the place where he lies (*Sanhedrin* 47b, *Yore Deah* 364:3).

But the burial in a national cemetery of bodies brought back to the United States, or of veterans who die after the war, such are not to be considered *mayss mitzvah,* and the question is, therefore, whether they must necessarily be buried in a Jewish cemetery or whether they may be buried in a national cemetery, such as Arlington or others. To this question this joint committee gave an open answer. It did not say it is forbidden, nor did it say outright that it was permitted. The reason for not forbidding such a burial in a national cemetery outright was that there is no definite law forbidding it. While it is true that it is a long-established custom in Jewish communities to have Jewish cemeteries, this is not a required law, although one or two scholars in recent generations have endeavored to raise this custom to the status of mandatory law (Eliezer Spiro, *Minchas Eliezer,* II, 41; also Eliezer Deutsch in *Dudoye Hasada,* #33, 66). Many small congregations all through Jewish history did not have a cemetery of their own but sent the bodies to a larger community. All that the law actually requires is that a man should be buried in his own property *(besoch shelo)* (*Baba Basra* 112a) and also that no righteous person should be buried by the side of a sinful one *(Sanhedrin* 47a). And as an actual fact, in ancient times in Palestine, there were family caves which were the

property of the family. Therefore the committee could not
say outright that it is forbidden for a Jewish soldier to be
buried anywhere else but in a Jewish cemetery. It left the
matter open for each family to consult its own rabbi, who
would decide the issue and whether he would officiate or
not. Of course, under this joint ruling, Reform rabbis and
many Conservative rabbis would permit burial in the
national cemetery and would officiate. But beyond this
general though indeterminate permissibility, there are
definite and positive reasons why a Reform and possibly a
Conservative rabbi would, without hesitation, permit such
burial and officiate at it. First of all, the national cemetery
belongs to the nation, and every Jewish citizen can be
declared as much an owner of it as any other citizen. If he is
buried there, the plot in which he is buried can certainly be
called *besoch shelo,* "in his own property." Besides, later
scholars have often described the Jewish cemetery as a
courtyard owned in partnership, *chotzer shel shutfin,* and
certainly all of us, Jews and Christians, are, as citizens,
partners in the national cemetery.

A further consideration is the fact that the national
cemetery, which belongs to us all, is in no sense a
Christian cemetery. The military services held over each
soldier—the bugles, the volley, etc.—are the same for
everyone. A Christian soldier may have a Christian
chaplain or minister, a Jewish soldier may have a Jewish
chaplain or rabbi. The national cemetery is as much Jewish
as it is Christian.

These, then, are the considerations relevant here. All
that the Jewish law actually requires is that a man should be
buried in his own property and not next to evildoers. On a

battlefield the grave is considered to be the property of the fallen soldier since he is a *mayss mitzvah*. Under non-battlefield conditions, a national cemetery belongs equally to every American citizen and is in no sense a Christian cemetery. Therefore no Reform and very few Conservative rabbis would deny the right or the propriety of a Jewish veteran to be buried in a national cemetery or would refuse to officiate for that reason.

26

CONGREGATION USING CEMETERY MONEY

QUESTION:

In Wheeling, West Virginia, there are three Jewish cemeteries which are privately owned and managed. The owners
now wish to turn these cemeteries over to the congregation.
However, they make the condition that none of the income
from the cemetery be used by the congregation for any other
than cemetery purposes. May the congregation accept this
restriction? If they accept it, may they, when circumstances
change later, use the money for other congregational purposes? (Asked by B.L. through M.S.)

ANSWER:

THE FACT THAT the cemetery owners have publicly
declared their intention of giving their cemetery property
over to the synagogue has, in itself, a certain importance in
Jewish law. It is deemed to be more or less in the nature of
a vow; and the question then becomes this: May one who
has announced a gift to a congregation change the purpose
or the recipient or the conditions of the gift? This question
is given its final decision in the *Shulchan Aruch (Yore
Deah* 259:1). It is as follows: As long as the gift has not
been formally transferred to the recipients (in this case, the
congregation), the owners may change its purposes or the
conditions of the gift, or even the recipient. In this case,
the announced intention of the owners to turn the

cemeteries over to the congregation does not obligate them to the letter of the condition until the property is actually formally received by the congregation *(Yore Deah* 259:1). Therefore, if the discussions between the donors and the congregation result in some sort of compromise, the conditions of the gift may well be changed. But if the congregation has already accepted the gift, it is difficult to change the agreed-upon conditions.

While difficult, it is not impossible even then (when the gift has already been formally accepted) to change the agreed-upon purposes under certain limited conditions. If the gift were, for example, a menorah given to the synagogue, or an Ark given to the synagogue, or a window, and the name of the donor is on the object or known to be associated with the object, then it is difficult to change the purpose for which it was given. Under these circumstances, the congregation may not sell the gift (e.g., the menorah) and use the money for some other congregational appurtenance. Therefore, if this gift of the cemetery remains associated with the names of the donors, it becomes more difficult to use some of the money, the income, for any other purpose. But, for example, if many years from now the names of the donors were forgotten, there would be almost no difficulty in the congregation using some of the money of the cemetery income for any other congregational purpose.

But we must assume that this possibility is highly theoretical. It is known, and will be known for quite some time, who were the donors of this cemetery gift. Nevertheless, even when the names of the donors are known and associated with the gift, it is still possible for the congregation to change the original stipulation that none of the money be used for other than cemetery purposes. But the question is, what changes, according to the spirit of Jewish law, may a congregation make in the original stipulations of the gift?

This question goes back to the time of the Mishnah. In Mishnah *Megillah* 3:1, we read that the officers may sell the city square (which was deemed a religious place because fast-day services were held there) to buy a synagogue. They may sell the synagogue to buy an Ark. They may sell an Ark to buy a Torah. The principle is derived here that in all such sales and purchases, the movement must be upward from the less holy to the more holy. This, then, is discussed in the Talmud, which tells us what is the most holy purpose of all for which any synagogue appurtenance may be sold or synagogue money may be used. In *Megillah* 27a the conclusion is that even a sacred Sefer Torah may be sold for the purpose of providing money for education. This is established as law in the *Shulchan Aruch* 259:2, which says specifically: "Money which has been donated for the needs of the synagogue, or for the needs of the cemetery, may be converted for the use of the school or the study of the Torah." In other words, no matter what are the conditions of the gift, they may always be changed by the congregation, but only for the purpose of Torah study. In our case that means helping the religious school or adult education. Isserles makes a partial modification of this rule, namely, that if education is already generally provided for, then of course such a change in the purpose of the original gift should not be made. But in general this rule stands.

This question has been discussed from Talmudic times on. Asher ben Yechiel (who left Germany at the time of the Crusades and settled in Spain) comes to this conclusion in his responsa (section 13, #14), and so do Joseph Colon (15th century, Italy; responsum #124) and, in modern times, Moses Feinstein (*Igros Moshe,* new series, *Orach Chayim* 26).

Perhaps the solution of the problem should be as follows: that the congregation and the donors agree that the cemetery income shall not be used for any congregational purpose except when needed for religious education, provided that there will always be sufficient funds left for cemetery uses.

Incidentally, as a matter of practical experience, many congregations use money from their cemetery for congregational purposes. Of course, they are not restricted since the cemetery money was not a gift to the congregation, as it is in this case.

Addendum

Subsequently to writing the above, I was informed that the congregation and the owners of the cemeteries have not yet come to an agreement. The owners insist that the money in the cemetery funds and income be used only for cemetery purposes, and the congregation feels that there are too many restrictions placed upon the proposed gift.

Clearly it is of considerable importance that both sides make an effort to come to an agreement. On the part of the present owners of the cemeteries, they must realize that

Jewish traditional law permits the transfer of some of such funds for educational purposes; that is to say, for Jewish religious educational purposes (Torah). But if, for example, the congregation conducts a class, as some congregations are doing, to teach English to newly arrived immigrants, it would not be permissible to use cemetery money for such a purpose. But for the religious school, for bringing lecturers for adult education, etc., it would be permissible. All this is stated and reiterated in the law. Then one might well say that this much of a concession the owners are not only permitted, but are required to make according to Jewish tradition.

As for the congregation and its board, they may well feel that too many restrictions are being placed on the gift. But they must also bear in mind that maintaining a Jewish cemetery is not the responsibility of private businessmen but of a congregation. All over the Jewish world, Jewish communities have been uneasy when they did not own the cemetery outright because princes and lords of the manor could desecrate the cemeteries by building roads through them. It is for that reason that the great Rabbi of Kovno two generations ago, Isaac Elchanan Spektor (in his responsa *Eyn Yitzchok, Yore Deah* 24), would not permit a burial in a cemetery which was not owned outright by the Jewish community. So the congregation surely is aware that to own a cemetery is a responsibility of the congregation.

Therefore it is clear that in spite of all difficulties, the spirit of the tradition remains, in this case, that both parties should make the necessary concessions so that a Jewish congregation can fulfill its responsibility and own a cemetery outright.

27

NOT USING THE CHEVRA KADISHA

QUESTION:

The congregation has a *Chevra Kadisha* which provides a *minyan* and a meal of consolation, etc., to the families of the bereaved. They perform this service both for members and non-members of the congregation. Some citizens, members or non-members, wish the funeral to be so private that they do not have the *Chevra Kadisha* participate. Have the people the right to do so? May the rabbi officiate at such funerals? (Asked by Rabbi Albert A. Michels, Sun City, Arizona.)

ANSWER:

IT MUST BE understood at the outset that the status of the *Chevra Kadisha* is different in the United States from what it was in the Old World. There the congregation or the various congregations were part of a united community, and the *Chevra Kadisha* was a communal organization. Therefore all members of the community had the right to the services of the *Chevra,* and the *Chevra* had the right to deal with all deaths. But even so, a person was not necessarily bound to turn the body over to the *Chevra,* as can be seen from the fact that many a time a body was buried in another city and the local *Chevra* had little to do with it except, perhaps, to aid in the transportation.

Here in America the Jews do not have one community,

but belong to separate congregations. Therefore, as far as non-members of the congregation are concerned, there can be no mutual obligation between them and the *Chevra* of a congregation to which they do not belong. As for members of the congregation, it may well be considered that when they joined the congregation, the implication was that they accepted the congregational constitution, which involves use of the *Chevra Kadisha*.

But even so, members of the congregation have rights with regard to the funeral arrangements, and, in fact, the deceased also has rights (as our father Jacob had the right to say where he would be buried). That right is clearly stated by Isserles in *Yore Deah* 362:2. Or a man may have the right to say he wants no eulogy. But no one, whether the deceased himself or his family, has the right to request anything that is contrary to Jewish law. For example, if a person left the request or the family makes the request that the body not be buried (as in the case of the modern plans of cryobiology), such requests, being contrary to Jewish law, are not to be heeded (*Yore Deah* 348:3).

Therefore the question comes down to whether what your *Chevra Kadisha* provides is *required* by Jewish law or is merely a custom. For example, is the *minyan* really required? True, of course, the mourner must stay at home for a week, although why is it not enough if he prays privately at home? Must there be a *minyan*? Isserles (*Yore Deah* 384:3) says it is a *mitzvah* to have these services at the home, but Joseph Caro does not mention it as a requirement. But we may count the *minyan*, therefore, as an established custom, at least among the Ashkenazim. As for bringing food to the bereaved, it is true that they may not eat their own food for the first meal; so that, too, may be counted as an established custom.

Therefore we may conclude that in America, where the *Chevra* is not communal but congregational, non-members are certainly not required to have its services. As for members, they have a stronger requirement to use the *Chevra,* but they, too, need not be mandated to observe whatever is not strictly a *mitzvah.*

As for the rabbi, it is his duty to officiate for all Jewish people, and he certainly cannot refuse. Even a Kohen must defile himself for a *mayss mitzvah,* and burying the dead has become, in America, a *mitzvah* incumbent upon the rabbi, especially if the family requests his service.

28

QUICKLIME ON THE BODY

QUESTION:

A congregant is frightened by a negative fantasy of bodily decomposition after death. For this reason she plans to be cremated. The only way she would agree to interment is if quicklime were to be sprinkled over her remains to speed decomposition. She makes this a condition for ground burial. What is your opinion of this practice? (Asked by Rabbi Sheldon W. Moss, San Diego, California.)

ANSWER:

YOUR QUESTION is whether, according to Jewish legal tradition, it is permissible to sprinkle quicklime over the remains to speed decomposition. I can answer you first indirectly. Speeding decomposition is definitely in accordance with the spirit of Jewish law. The rabbis had to explain away the fact that the body of Joseph was embalmed to delay decomposition. More positively, they are in favor of direct contact of the body with the earth to hasten decomposition. Therefore it is only with difficulty that they have come to permit coffins at all.

Now, more specifically, there is a responsum (#389) by the great Spanish authority Solomon ben Aderet as follows: A dying man asked his sons to bury him in the family plot in Oran, but he died in Algiers, and there was a war going on, so it was unsafe to transport the body and he was buried in Algiers. After a brief period the sons asked the rabbi whether they might disinter their father's body. to fulfill his dying wish and bury him in Oran. However, the body was only partially decomposed and could not be handled. They asked, therefore, whether they might put quicklime on the remains to complete the decomposition of the flesh. The rabbi gave his full consent to this. In fact, you may say that putting lime on the body to hasten decay has virtually become a Jewish custom among certain traditions in Jewish life. Note the following:

Isserles (in *Yore Deah* 363:2) says, "It is permitted to put lime upon him in order to hasten the decay of the flesh." Jacob Reischer, the famous Rabbi of Metz (1870), in his *Shevus Yaacov* (II, #97), speaks of a case in which the government prohibited burial in the Jewish cemetery and buried the dead out in the field. He recommended that they follow the precedent of Solomon ben Aderet to put lime on the body so that they would be able to transfer it to the security of the regular Jewish cemetery. In fact, it has become a custom, especially among the Sephardim, to follow the practice of using quicklime.

So you see that Jewish tradition opposes anything which delays decomposition of the flesh, and, specifically, great rabbis gave their clear permission to hasten decomposition by the use of quicklime.

29

POST-FUNERAL EULOGY

QUESTION:

In this retirement-community congregation, relatives of a person who dies often make funeral arrangements in the original home of the deceased. Then, when the family returns to the retirement community, they would like to have a memorial service with a eulogy in the presence of their new friends. Is this extra eulogy (perhaps with a service) permissible according to the Jewish legal tradition? (From Rabbi Albert A. Michels, Sun City, Arizona.)

ANSWER:

FIRST OF ALL, the general attitude of the law to the giving of eulogies is closely relevant to the question asked here. The Talmud in *Shabbat* 105b (and codified in the *Shulchan Aruch, Yore Deah* 344) considers the giving of the eulogy a great *mitzvah,* and indeed, it is even permitted to overstate (to some extent) the virtues of the deceased. It is even deemed to be a sin to *neglect* giving an adequate eulogy. So, therefore, one may say that as a general attitude, giving more than one eulogy would be considered a *mitzvah* rather than a superfluity.

Actually, one does not need to rely upon this general mood as to eulogies. A rule with regard to eulogies is that they are not permitted within thirty days of one of the festivals. This is derived from the Talmud, *Moed Katan* 8a. The reason for this is to prevent a mood of gloom darkening the happiness of the festival. However, it is permitted to ignore this rule for a special eulogy for a scholar, and in discussing this, Joseph Caro to the *Bes Joseph* in *Yore Deah,* end of 344, says (describing a general custom) that people would gather in special assemblies in the month of Adar and Elul to learn the laws governing the forthcoming festivals, and at these gatherings it was customary to give eulogies for scholars. So he says specifically, in *Orach Chayim* 347:5, that it is the custom to have the eulogies for a worthy person even within thirty days of the festival. The matter of the additional eulogies is discussed by various scholars, especially by Jacob Reischer of Metz in his *Shevus Yaacov* (II, #25). So it is clear that the custom of additional eulogies long after a man's funeral was an established custom.

As for the distinction between eulogizing scholars and average people, that distinction is fading. Often in the law they mention that the special status and privilege of a scholar is no longer to be maintained. Also, there is frequent mention of the fact that the average Jewish man is to be considered one who knows, if not the Talmud, then Mishnah or Scripture (and is scholarly). My own congregation, even though the law was known that only scholars and leaders of the community should be eulogized or their funeral conducted from the main sanctuary, nevertheless decided that any member whose family so desires shall be buried from the main sanctuary of the temple. While this is not in accordance with the strict letter of the law (see references in *Reform Responsa for Our Time,* pp. 95 ff.), it is in harmony with the general tendency of equality in Jewish law.

To sum up: In general, the giving of eulogy is highly praised in the tradition. Therefore, additional eulogies are in accordance with the spirit of the law. In fact, specifically, frequent mention is made of repeated eulogies given long after the man's death, and in general we need not emphasize so much the difference between the scholarly and the unscholarly.

Addendum

Subsequently, an additional question was asked with regard to the post-funeral eulogy, namely, whether it would be proper to give the later eulogies at the Sabbath service.

At first it would seem inappropriate to have any type of funeral service or eulogy or memorial prayers on the Sabbath, when it is a duty to rejoice *(Oneg Shabbas)*. Yet in spite of this doubt as to the propriety of marring the happiness of the Sabbath, the custom of having memorial prayers on the Sabbath has grown up over the centuries. Actually, memorial prayers for the dead, which originated in the Rhineland, were given only on Yom Kippur, but then they spread from Yom Kippur to the last days of the three joyous festivals, Passover, Shavuos, and Succos *(Yizkor)*. The *Yizkor* memorial prayer certainly might be looked upon as marring the mood of the festival, since we are commanded, "Thou shalt rejoice on thy festivals." Nevertheless, the custom became established to have the prayer on these days, perhaps because the prayer is not only sorrowful, but also brings certain consolation and peace to the heart.

So finally it was with the Sabbath; it became an established custom to have the prayer *Av Ho-Rachamim,* a prayer memorializing all the martyrs, on every Sabbath after the Torah reading. The German congregations recite this prayer on only two Sabbaths of the year, the Sabbath before Shavuos and the Sabbath before Tishe B'av, but the Eastern European congregations recite it on every Sabbath (with certain exceptions, such as the Sabbath on which the New Moon is blessed, but even on such a Sabbath, according to some authorities, prayers for the dead are permitted for those who died during the week).

It is not only these special prayers for the martyrs that are recited in the Sabbath service. The memorial prayers are considered prayers for the *welfare* of the departed and therefore are grouped together by the authorities with other prayers which are for the welfare of the living.

Perhaps the earliest source for the recital of such prayers for the dead and for the living is the *Shibbole Ha-Leket* by Zedukiah Anaw (Italy, 12th century). From this source (ed. Buber, p. 29b, sec. 81), many of the leading authorities quote the custom of praying for the dead and for the welfare of the living who have served the congregation and the community (Joseph Caro, in his *Bes Joseph* to *Orach Chayim* 284, and in the *Shulchan Aruch,* Isserles 284:7). Such prayers have become a formal and fixed part of the prayerbook to be recited after the Haftorah, namely, the *Mi Sheberach* and the *Av Ho-Rachamim.*

Besides these fixed prayers of memorial and welfare found in the prayerbooks, similar prayers were also given in a sort of extemporaneous manner when each individual was called up to the Torah. The reader would recite a *Mi Sheberach* in his behalf, blessing him for contributions to the synagogue, cantor, etc., or voicing a prayer for a sick person or for a woman in childbirth.

The custom of memorial and welfare, either for an individual when called to the Torah or as fixed prayers for the entire congregation after the Torah reading, all these are adequate justification for the additional memorial eulogy asked about here being given on the Sabbath. However, since the question comes from a modern Reform-type of congregation, the place in the service of these prayers and this eulogy must be different from the place in the service customary in an Orthodox congregation. It is not the custom in Reform congregations to call up seven people to the Torah, and therefore the needs of various worshipers can hardly arise as part of the Torah reading. But it has become a well-established custom in Reform congregations to have a memorial prayer before the *Kaddish,* and in general the entire congregation joins in the *Kaddish* as an expression of mutual fellowship in sorrow. Some congregations also mention the names of the recently deceased at that time. Therefore, if such an additional eulogy would be given in the Sabbath service, the appropriate time would be, not after the Torah reading, as in Orthodox synagogues, but before the *Kaddish*.

Nevertheless, one or two words of general caution should be mentioned. The authorities are indeed concerned that the mood of the Sabbath should not be marred by such eulogies or memorials, and therefore the statement is made that no tragic or tearful eulogies be given on the

Sabbath but only eulogies of an edifying nature honoring the departed for his character and his good deeds, to serve as an example to his family and the community (see especially Greenwald, *Kol Bo,* p. 104, #24).

Another concern must also be mentioned besides that of avoiding the mood of tragedy, namely, the concern as to unduly lengthening the service and thus making it a burden on the congregation. Burdening the congregation *(torach ha-tzibbur)* is always to be guarded against. So the leading authority on the laws around the Torah reading, Ephraim Margolis *(Sha'ar Ephraim,* Gate 4 #24), specifically says that the prayers of memorial and welfare should be kept short so as not to be a "burden to the congregation."

This whole matter depends upon local customs, as Isserles says in his Note to the *Shulchan Aruch* (ibid.): "Every place follows its own customs in this matter." Therefore, if the eulogies are likely to be too sorrowful, and if the service might be unduly lengthened by them, the congregation has the right to establish its own custom and might very well establish a special service for this purpose on Sunday morning; or, since this is a retirement community, the service could be established at any time during the week.

Nevertheless, it is clear that if the eulogies are not too tearful, but serve as an edification to the community, and if they do not unduly lengthen the service, there is no objection to their taking place as part of the Sabbath service; in fact, there is established custom in support of it.

30

SHIVA IN JERUSALEM

QUESTION:

A man expressed his dying wish to be buried in Jerusalem. His son in San Francisco will accompany the body to Jerusalem for burial. The family, however, as did the deceased, lives in New York, and there they will sit *shiva,* etc. The son who is accompanying the body understands that his own mourning should begin with the burial, but is he required to carry out the *shiva* and the *shloshim* in Jerusalem or may he join the family in New York? (Asked by J.T., San Francisco, California.)

ANSWER:

THE QUESTION that you asked me over the telephone is not too easy to answer. If it were simple and clear-cut, you would not have needed to ask it at all. Yet it is strange that it *should* be difficult. After all, the circumstances upon which the question is based, namely, moving a body from one city or from one country to another, have occurred innumerable times in Jewish experience, and, in fact, the law is quite clear-cut on most of the elements involved. Most of it, of course, is stated in the *Tur* and in the *Shulchan Aruch (Yore Deah* 375:2). Yet nearly all the details dealt with concern the question of *when* the mourning begins. On that question the general consensus, as established in law, is that the people who are in the city

of departure begin their mourning when the body leaves
them to go on its journey. But those people who accompany the body do not begin their mourning until the body is
actually buried.

All this seems clear enough, but what is omitted is
exactly the content of your question. What about the
mourning duties of those who accompany the body? Are
they expected to sit *shiva* and observe *shloshim* in a strange
city, as in this case in Jerusalem? What should, for
example, this American visitor do who accompanies his
parent's body for burial in Jerusalem? Is he expected to
rent living quarters and observe *shiva* and *shloshim* in
Jerusalem after the burial? This human difficulty is not
clear at all in the law and is really the essence of the
question.

How, then, can we decide in this humanly difficult
situation? It is well enough for the law to tell us that the
mourning for this American begins in Jerusalem after the
burial, but must he observe the mourning period there or
not?

In all cases where the law is not specific, the answer
must be derived by analogy, or by the implications of the
law. Perhaps it can be found in a closer look at the laws of
the two separate mourning dates in such cases.

An early discussion of this question is found in the
Tosfos to *Moed Katan* 22a. There the rule is stated as we
know it—that those at home begin when the body leaves,
and those with the body begin when it is buried. But then
the *Tosfos* follows with a complication of this clear rule,
namely, that it all depends on whether the *godol
hamishpocha,* the head of the household (the one upon

whom the household depends), stays at home or goes with the body. If it is he who goes with the body, then all the mourners, wherever they are, count from the time of burial, not from the time when the body leaves. However, the *Tosfos* then continues to indicate that the Yerushalmi differs in this matter. As a matter of fact, there is some doubt as to the proper version of the text in the Yerushalmi. A detailed attempt to clarify this confusion is to be found in Joseph Caro's *Bes Joseph* to the *Tur, Yore Deah* 375.

All this has some relevance to our question. Akiba Eger, in his comment to the *Shulchan Aruch* at this point, tries to clarify the above difficulty as to the head of the household's presence or absence. He says that whether they count from the departure of the body or from the burial does indeed depend on where the head of the household is, but that this must be modified as follows: Everybody follows the time of burial if the head of the household goes along with the body, *provided* the head of the household is taking the body to be buried in his (i.e., the head of the household's) hometown. Then, of course, he stays there and observes *shiva* and *shloshim*. If, however, the funeral is not in the hometown of the head of the household (i.e., if the head of the household is a stranger there), he returns to where the family is mourning (i.e., to the city of departure) and joins them, and even if he comes on the seventh day of *shiva*, their observance counts for him and he does not need to observe *shiva* any further. I have here rather amplified Akiba Eger's answer, which is rather terse, but this is clearly his meaning. (Akiba Eger's opinion is not just his own; it was based on the *Shach,* end of section 12 to *Yore Deah* 375:8.)

Even though the son who is accompanying the body in the case which you mentioned is not "the head of the household," Akiba Eger's rule clearly applies to him. In fact it applies to him all the more. If "the head of the household" need not observe *shiva* and *shloshim* at the place of burial, then he who is not head of the household certainly need not do so. Jerusalem is not his hometown. He is not required to rent quarters to stay there during a long mourning period. He can come back and join the family and share in their *shiva*. This is a practical answer, especially nowadays, since burial takes place almost immediately in Jerusalem and the man can be back in America in two or three days. Even if it took him seven days (scant), it would still be fulfillment of the law of *shiva*.

Of course, this must be added: The son in Jerusalem stands by at the burial of his father. Is there *nothing* that he needs to observe at all? There is the possibility of some observance which he may feel the need to follow. In the laws of *Likkut Atzomos,* i.e., the reburial of a body as described in the *Shulchan Aruch, Yore Deah* 403:12, a son at such a time is required to observe the ritual of *keriah* and mourn for one day. This, then, would seem to be the proper answer as derivable from the lack of present clarity in the law. The son, not going to his hometown, need not stay for *shiva* and *shloshim,* but may rejoin the family. This is quite practical nowadays with air travel, and even if one day of *shiva* is left, this is a fulfillment of his obligation. In Jerusalem he may observe *keriah* and mourn for one day before returning home.

This suggestion as to *keriah* and one-day mourning at

the burial has precedence in an analogous case mentioned from earlier sources in Greenwald's *Kol Bo,* p. 299, where a family had started its mourning after the body left the city and the body was confiscated or, we might say, kidnapped by the authorities for ransom. Afterwards they got the body and buried it, and the decision was that those present at the burial mourn one day, just as in case of *Likkut Atzomos* (see also *Derisha* [Joshua Falk] to *Tur, Yore Deah* 375:3).

31

COMFORTING THE BEREAVED ON THE SABBATH

QUESTION:

Certain members of our congregation believe that it is contrary to Jewish law and custom to call on the bereaved to comfort them on the Sabbath. Is this actually so? (Asked by Rabbi Joseph Narot, Miami, Florida.)

ANSWER:

THE PEOPLE who are under the impression that it is contrary to Jewish law or custom to visit the bereaved on the Sabbath are not entirely mistaken. They have either memories or traditions of some local custom to that effect. As a matter of fact, Yechiel Epstein, in his *Aruch Ha-Shulchan* (*Orach Chayim* 387:3) discusses the matter and ends his statement by saying, "In our city [Novorodok] it is not the custom to visit the bereaved on the Sabbath." The well-known Chassidic leader of the past generation, Eliezer Spiro (Der Muncaczer), author of the responsa *Minchas Eliezer,* also wrote notes to the *Shulchan Aruch, Orach Chayim (Nimuke Orach Chayim).* I do not have this work with me, but it is quoted by a number of authorities (e.g., Greenwald in *Kol Bo,* p. 298) as having said, "If people were more worthy, it would be better if they did not visit the bereaved on the

Sabbath." Nevertheless, Spiro does not record (as Epstein did) any actual local custom not to visit the bereaved on the Sabbath.

A local custom in a respected community usually has some basis. In this case, the basis is the general objection to any lamentation or expressions of sorrow on Sabbath or holidays. No penitential prayers *(Tachanun)* are recited on the Sabbath and holidays. But in addition to this general objection to any expression of sorrow on the Sabbath, there is a specific statement in the Talmud against such Sabbath visitation. In tractate *Sabbath* 12a, the school of Shammai says that we may not visit the sick or go to comfort the mourners on the Sabbath. This clear prohibition is, of course, based upon the general objection to lamentations and sad prayers on the Sabbath and holidays. But the prohibition is the opinion only of the school of Shammai. The school of Hillel, however, says that we *may* visit the sick and go to comfort the mourners on Sabbath and holidays.

Of course, since the school of Shammai bases its objection to such visitation on the general avoidance of lamentations and sadness on the Sabbath, there is some concession made in the Talmud to their prohibition. It is as follows: You may visit the sick on the Sabbath, as the school of Hillel says, but you must utter a special formula as follows: "It is the Sabbath; we may not lament, but healing will surely come." And in fact, some of the later authorities suggest a similar formula when comforting the mourners, as follows: "It is the Sabbath; we may not actively console, but God's consolation will surely come" (see *Magen Avraham* to *Orach Chayim* 287). Maimonides

permits visiting the sick and comforting mourners on the
Sabbath (*Yad, Hil. Shabbat* 24:5). The *Shulchan Aruch*
(*Orach Chayim* 287 and *Yore Deah* 399:2) states clearly
that (whatever formula is used) we *may* go and comfort the
mourners on the Sabbath and holidays. The *Magen Avraham* voices some objection to those who refrain from
calling on the mourners during weekdays but visit *only* on
the Sabbath; but the *Be'er Hetev* brushes that objection
aside and considers it a special *mitzvah* to come on the
Sabbath.

The latest codification of the laws of mourning (Greenwald, in his *Kol Bo,* p. 298) says simply that we comfort
the mourners on Sabbath, and he gives an interesting
justification from Talmud *Succah* 41b. There we are told
that the men of Jerusalem, on the festival of Succos, would
go to the synagogue carrying their *lulavim,* pray the holiday
service, then leave the synagogue, carrying their *lulavim,*
and go to comfort the mourners.

So, to sum up: The general objection to expressions of
sadness on Sabbath and holidays is the basis of the school
of Shammai's prohibition of visiting the sick and comforting the mourners on the Sabbath. But the school of
Hillel disagrees; and the law is according to them, except
that on the Sabbath and holidays we avoid too somber a
mood during the visit. Whatever objection there may be
about visiting the mourners on the Sabbath has found
expression in a local custom or two. But this is not the law
or the general practice.

32

VISITING THE BEREAVED

QUESTION:

In the last decade or so, a considerable change has come about in the manner and timing in which people visit the bereaved. It is now a growing custom for people to pay their condolence call at the funeral parlor (or wherever the funeral is to be held). The call is paid before the funeral service. Although Orthodox authorities strongly object to it, this custom has by now become widespread. What is the actual situation in law and custom with regard to the proper time for visiting the bereaved? (Asked by Rabbi Mark Staitman, Pittsburgh, Pennsylvania.)

ANSWER:

THE MODERN change in the visiting of the bereaved has become widespread and often supplants the visitation in the home during the seven days of mourning. Quite understandably, Orthodox authorities object to this development. It tends to abolish the sitting of *shiva* at home and therefore makes almost impossible the six days of home service which tradition requires. Besides the fact that the new customs make seven days of *shiva* virtually impossible, the rabbis would have two other objections to this new custom. First, it takes place before the burial, and before the burial the bereaved is still an *onayn,* not yet an *ovel,* i.e., a mourner who is to be consoled. There should be no attempt at consolation before the burial. Second, psychologically, such visits might be futile, as the rabbis say in the *Ethics of the Fathers* (4:23): "Do not comfort a man while his dead still lies before him," which means, of course, that since the dead is not even buried yet, words of consolation are too premature to have any consoling effect.

Clearly, then, this modern change in funeral obser- vances among many American Jews, Reform and Conser- vative, requires careful study, for evidently the custom will continue and even spread. This is highly probable, first of all, because more and more people live in apart- ments rather than in private houses, so it becomes difficult to have large numbers of people visiting. Also, families nowadays are scattered over the country, and often rela- tives come just for the funeral. Therefore the only time their friends and well-wishers can see them is at the funeral parlor before they go back to their distant homes.

Since this new practice is a result of an unchangeable social situation, it would be almost hopeless to try to stop it. Thus it might perhaps be wise to follow the rabbinical dictum not to make a decision when we know beforehand that it will not be obeyed (*Yevamos* 65b). Under these circumstances it becomes necessary to restudy the various laws involved in the visiting of the bereaved and to see to what extent, or with what possible modification, the present situation can perhaps be considered acceptable.

It must be understood at the outset that the consoling of the bereaved is held to be an outstandingly important *mitzvah,* in fact, it is deemed to be an *imitatio dei*. The Talmud in *Sota* 14a says that God comforted Isaac when he was bereaved. This is based upon Genesis 25:18, which states that after Abraham died, God brought His blessing to Isaac. Developing this verse, the Talmud says that just as God comforts the mourners, so do thou also comfort the mourners. Also, the *Avoth of Rabbi Nathan* (ed. Schechter, chap. 30) says that whoever comforts the mourners brings a blessing to all the world. Since, therefore, this *mitzvah* is so highly valued, then as a general policy we should be inclined to encourage the observance of this *mitzvah* whenever it may be possible for it to be performed. The question remains, however, as to what are the actual limitations in the Halachah to the performing of this *mitzvah*.

As a matter of fact, because of the great worth of this *mitzvah,* the Halachah permits it to be performed even under circumstances in which one might have anticipated it would not be permitted. For example, it is important not to let anything mar the joy of the Sabbath. One would think that visiting the bereaved would be prohibited on the Sabbath because of the sadness it would engender in the visitor. And, indeed, Rabbi Chanina says (*Shabbat* 12b) that it was with reluctance *(b'kushi)* that they permitted visiting the bereaved on the Sabbath. With reluctance indeed, but they *permitted* it. In this decision they follow the school of Hillel against the school of Shammai, which, indeed, would have prohibited it (ibid. 12a). And so it is recorded in the *Shulchan Aruch (Orach Chayim* 287:1), where the law plainly says that we may comfort mourners on the Sabbath (also Maimonides, *Hil. Shabbos* 24:5). The *Magen Avraham* makes an interesting comment to this general permission, namely, that this permission should

not be used as an encouragement to those who stay away
from the mourners all week but come only on the Sabbath
(presumably when their businesses are closed and there is
no work). However, Yechiel Epstein (*Aruch Ha-
Shulchan*, ad loc.) would permit people to visit on the
Sabbath if they really had no time to visit because of
business or work during the week. But be that as it may,
visiting the bereaved on the Sabbath *is* permitted. As a
matter of fact, while the mourner may go to the synagogue
on Friday night, the services in his house are expected to
last for seven days, which would, of course, include the
presence of consoling visitors on the Sabbath too. So it is
permitted also to perform the *mitzvah* of consolation on
holidays. We are told (*b. Succah* 41b) that the pious men of
Jerusalem went from the synagogue on Succos and, with
their *lulavs* in their hands, paid visits of consolation on the
bereaved (see the full discussion in Greenwald's *Kol Bo*,
pp. 297–99).

While the law thus acknowledges the special worth of
this *mitzvah* (i.e., by extending it to Sabbath and holidays), the people themselves, in past generations, have
developed customs of the opposite tendency—namely, to
restrict the permissibility of these visits (contrary to the
Halachah). Some people believe that the mourners should
not be visited for the first three days of the seven. This
notion is based upon the Midrashic idea (*Leviticus R*. 18:1)
that the soul of the dead hovers around the body for three
days. Others believe that the mourners should not be
visited on the first day of the *shiva* (cf. *Ginze Joseph* 74:2,
where the author, Joseph Schwartz, proves that there is no
Halachic justification for this). But all these folk-created

restrictions have no foundation in law, as can be seen from the fact that originally the mourners were consoled right at the cemetery, immediately after the burial. In fact, an elaborate ceremony was developed there in which the friends stood in two parallel lines and the mourners passed between them (right at the graveside) to be consoled (*Tur, Yore Deah* 376). Indeed it was expected, also, that friends would accompany the mourners from the cemetery and go right to their house to console them after the funeral (*Maharil,* responsum #23), and also, of course, to help with the first meal, which must be provided by friends. Greenwald also quotes the famous Chassidic authority of the last generation, Eliezer Spiro, who observed the fact that some people avoid calling on the bereaved on Sabbath and holidays and said, "Has the generation become so righteous that it now does not console the mourners on Sabbath and holidays?" This (sarcastic) phrase, "has the generation become so righteous," is derived from the discussion of *yibbum* vs. *chalitza* in *Yevamos* 39b, and the opening phrase must be read as a (scornful) question (see Rashi ad loc.).

Of course, there still remains the objection that the modern custom of visiting the bereaved takes place *before* the burial, when the formal mourning *(avelus)* has not yet begun. But even with regard to this fact, there is at least one circumstance of permissibility, and it derives from a special case discussed by the Gaon Hai. The Gaon is quoted by Ibn Yarchi (12th century) in his *Ha-Manhig* in the laws of *Esrog,* #32, where he speaks of the following special case: If a man dies during the holiday and he is buried, the *avelus* does not begin until after the holiday.

Yet, although the *avelus* has not even begun, friends of the bereaved, according to Gaon Hai, may visit them and make them feel calmer. In other words, here the Gaon speaks of visits to bring consolation even before the formal mourning, *avelus,* actually began.

In general we may say, therefore, that we are confronted with a social situation that is fairly irreversible, and since the *mitzvah* of consoling the bereaved is so great, we should take advantage of every element in the law which might permit us to condone it, lest by overstrictness we might discourage people altogether from coming to console the bereaved.

33

MOURNING FOR THE CREMATED

If a body has been cremated, are the relatives in duty bound to carry out the regular mourning, *shiva,* etc.? Or if they are not in duty bound, *may* they do so if they wish? (Asked by Rabbi Jack Segal, Houston, Texas.)

ANSWER:

ONE WOULD expect that this question would be definitely decided in the Halachah, yet actually it must be considered as still an open question. The reason for the indefiniteness on the matter is due to the fact that the status of the act of cremation and the question of the burial of the ashes in the cemetery have not been definitely decided. The most extreme opinion on this question was expressed by Rabbi Meyer Lerner in his book *Chaye Olom,* published in Berlin, 1904. At that time, apparently, the practice of cremation was beginning to spread in Germany among certain circles of Jewry. Thereupon Rabbi Lerner gathered opinions from the leading Orthodox rabbis, mostly of Eastern Europe, who answered entirely in the negative. Lerner himself, in the conclusion which he drew from all these negative opinions, came to the following outright decision, which he expressed in the last two pages of his book: Cremation, he said, is absolutely forbidden; the

ashes may not be buried in the Jewish cemetery, and
people who provide for the cremation of their bodies are
undoubtedly complete sinners with regard to Jewish ritual
and morality and belief. Therefore, no mourning at all
should be made for them.

It is evident that this is the most extreme possible
opinion on this matter. Michael Higger, at the end of his
book *Halachas v'Aggados,* has a long essay (beginning on
p. 161) proving that the out-and-out objection to cremation
is not quite justified according to the Halachah. Of course,
cremation ought not to be practiced, he says, because it is
contrary to established Jewish custom. But, he says, what
is actually forbidden is only the burning of a body in order
to disgrace it, but not if it is meant for the honor of
the deceased. Of course, no Orthodox authority would
openly permit cremation. Nevertheless, the fact that the
prohibition is not so clear-cut is evident from the fact that
other Orthodox authorities, such as Benamozegh of
Leghorn and David Hoffmann of Berlin, both permit the
burial of the ashes in the Jewish cemetery (see *Reform
Responsa for Our Time,* pp. 112 ff.).

Even from the point of view of the Halachah, which
must be considered as opposed to cremation, it would be
difficult to justify the extreme opinion of Meyer Lerner
that no mourning at all should be conducted for the
cremated. Let us say that the cremated person himself had
said that he wanted no regular funeral ritual. Even so, it
would be doubtful whether the survivors may dispense
with the mourning. The fact of the matter is that a man may
say he wants no elaborate funeral, and his wishes must
be acceded to because the funeral oration is considered to

be an act of homage or honor to the deceased, and the man, if he so wishes, may dispense with such honors. He may say, ''I do not want them.'' But the mourning, *shiva*, etc., are not merely an act of honor with which he may dispense. The mourning ritual is a religious duty incumbent upon the survivors. The deceased had no right to prohibit his survivors from performing a religious duty which is incumbent upon them. See the whole discussion in *Recent Reform Responsa,* especially p. 111, and particularly the responsum of Jacob Weill, #17, and the *Shulchan Aruch, Yore Deah* 344:10. There Joseph Caro states that if a man asks that no eulogy be made for him, we obey his request. To which Isserles adds that if, however, he asks that the seven and thirty days mourning be omitted, we do *not* obey his request. Therefore, even from the point of view of Orthodoxy, the opinion of Meyer Lerner that no mourning at all should be conducted is to be considered an extreme one. It is to be noticed that Greenwald (in his *Kol Bo,* pp. 54 ff.) merely cites Lerner's harsh opinion in quotation marks and does not state it as law.

The above is, of course, the situation in Orthodox law. But in Reform, our Central Conference decided long ago that no ritual should be omitted in the case of cremation (*CCAR Yearbook,* 1892, p. 43). We bury the ashes in our cemetery without question, and certainly, from our point of view, full mourning should be observed.

34

BODY LOST BUT FOUND LATER

QUESTION:

A man was drowned in a reservoir. The authorities have been searching for the body for a number of days. The search has been unsuccessful. The body cannot be found. What should be the funeral and mourning ritual procedure in this case? Furthermore, if the body does reappear later, what will be the ritual procedure then? (Asked by Rabbi Norman S. Lipson, Hattiesburg, Mississippi.)

ANSWER:

THE QUESTION is in two parts, first as to what is the procedure when a body is drowned and cannot be found, and second, what would be the procedure if, let us say, months later the body appears.

As for the first part of the question, with regard to a body that disappears in a river, a lake, or the ocean, the law in general is fairly clear. It is stated first in the post-Talmudic booklet *Semachos* (Vol. II, #11), namely, that if a body is drowned in a river and cannot be found, the family begins its regular mourning (seven and thirty days, etc.) from the moment they despair of finding the body *(mi-she-nis-yo-ashu)*. That moment of despair is taken to be the substitute for an actual burial. Just as mourning begins when the body is buried, so in the case of drowning, the mourning begins when the family gives up hope.

This question was discussed rather fully in *Reform Responsa* (pp. 147 ff.), where certain variations of the law are also given, namely, whether it is a man or a woman who is drowned, whether the man was married or not (on which the widow's right to remarry depends), and more importantly for our special question, whether the waters in which the drowning took place are "limited" (so that one could see the shoreline) or "unlimited," like the ocean. This (as to "limited" or "unlimited") is based upon the Mishnah *Yevamos* 16:4, and the Talmud 121b. In the case of "unlimited" waters, the man who is presumed drowned may perhaps have saved himself and may be, for all we know, safe on a distant island. Therefore the law is stricter about a woman being permitted to remarry if the supposed drowning was in "unlimited" waters and also, therefore, stricter about prohibiting the formal family mourning, which would be tantamount to a public declaration that she *is* truly a widow, a fact which is as yet uncertain. However, if it is "limited" water, as in this case, then whether it be a man or a woman who was drowned, there is no question that the formal mourning begins when hope is given up for the recovery of the body.

Now as to the second half of the question: What should be done ritually if, as sometimes happens a month or two following a drowning, the body reemerges and is found after all the formal mourning (after an optional memorial service)? This specific situation is rarely mentioned in the Halachah. But there are a number of analogous situations in the law which are sufficient to guide us.

First of all, as a general guide, in all debatable circumstances with regard to death and mourning, there must always be borne in mind the principle enunciated by Rabbi Samuel in *Moed Katan* 26b, namely, that when there is a disagreement as to what the procedure should be with regard to a situation involving mourning, the law is always in accordance with the more lenient decision *(halachah k'makil b'ovel)*. It will be noticed that this principle of leniency is actually followed in many situations contained in the law which are analogous to the question asked here. In the *Shulchan Aruch, Yore Deah* 375:3, the following law is given: If a body had been buried and mourning had begun, and then for some reason the body is disinterred and reburied in another grave, the family does not need to begin mourning again. The first mourning is sufficient. In fact, even if the burial in the first grave was with the announced intention of later burying the deceased elsewhere in another grave (for example, in his native city, when the opportunity would arise)—even then, in spite of the original intention, if the disinterment occurred after seven days, the family does not need to mourn again. Another case illustrating the leniency principle is given in 375:4. It is as follows: Normally, when a body is taken to another city for burial, the family in the first city begins mourning once the body leaves. In the second city (the destination), the mourning, of course, begins once the body is buried. But suppose—as, alas, often happened—the body was confiscated by the authorities on its journey and the family does not know when they can get the body for burial; nevertheless, having begun their mourning (in the original city), they do not need to mourn again *(Yore Deah* 375:7, Isserles).

There is only one circumstance under which some

mourning must be repeated, and that is if the son of the deceased (or, for that matter, any other of the seven close relatives) actually finds the body himself or is present when it is found. Then he and, some would say, the family must sit *shiva* for one hour and mourn for one day. So, too, if they are informed of the exact hour of discovery.

This requirement (needing to sit *shiva* for an hour and mourn for a day) is derived from the law in *Shulchan Aruch, Yore Deah* 403, in the laws of "gathering the bones," which means, the reburial of a body. Even in such a case of reburial, the great authority Moses Sofer practiced Samuel's principle of leniency. In his responsa, #353, he is asked about an order by the authorities for the Jewish community to vacate a certain cemetery, to remove all the bodies. By the law in the *Shulchan Aruch,* all the families, knowing the exact hour of the disinterment of their relatives, would need to sit *shiva* for that hour. Thereupon, Moses Sofer decreed that the *Chevra Kadisha* be forbidden to inform the community when the disinterment would take place, so that they should not need to sit *shiva* for the hour and mourn that day.

All this is applicable in the case mentioned. First of all, the drowning took place in "limited" waters. There is no doubt that the mourning begins the moment the family gives up hope, and this moment can be fixed by a memorial service if desired. If the body reemerges, let us say a month later, it is not likely that a son will be present at that moment, nor is it likely that the family will be informed that day (because of the need for official identification). Even if the son happened to be present at the actual reappearance of the body or if the family were informed that very day—all of which is highly improbable—then even so, we follow the unquestioned authority of Moses Sofer and have no ritual at all.

This is clearly the intention and the spirit of the law. If the body is found, it should be quietly buried. At the burial there is no objection to saying *Kaddish,* which may be said at any time, but otherwise no mourning ritual for the family is required.

Addendum

This situation finds occasional mention in the Halachah (see *Tur* 375). So, too, Joshua Falk, in his commentary to the *Tur* above (*Derisha,* para. 3), says that when the body is recovered, no repetition of the mourning ritual is required. Greenwald, in his *Kol Bo* (p. 299), speaks of such a case mentioned by the *Hagahos Smak.*

35

IS A TOMBSTONE MANDATORY?

QUESTION:

The question has arisen in our community whether it is necessary to have a tombstone on a grave. Does the law or the tradition clearly require it? (Asked by Rabbi Murray Blackman, New Orleans, Louisiana.)

ANSWER:

THERE ARE MANY references to tombstones or monuments in the literature, beginning with the Bible itself. Yet in spite of all these references, it is not clear whether to have a tombstone is a definite requirement of the law. The whole matter of the tombstone is considerably confused, and therefore, if we are to arrive at the responsibility of the family of the deceased, it is necessary to go into the subject historically and rather fully.

There are three references in the Bible. One is Genesis 38:20. Jacob put a monument on the grave of Rachel. The second reference is in II Kings 23:17. King Josiah, while on campaign, saw a tombstone *(tziun),* a marker, on a grave and was told that it marked the grave of a prophet. The third reference is in Ezekiel 39:15, where we are told that after the great wars, officials went through the land to purify it, and where they saw the bones or the body of a man, they put a marker there.

The Hungarian authority Moses Schick (Maharam Schick), in his responsa (*Yore Deah* 171), says that the Biblical references indicate that it was an unbroken tradition from Biblical times to have tombstones on the grave. But the Talmud (*Moed Katan* 5a) says that the custom is not based upon what Jacob did or King Josiah saw, but is learned from the reference of Ezekiel.

Broyde, in his article on "Tombstones" in the *Jewish Encyclopedia,* says that tombstones were unknown in the early days, and that the Jews of Palestine borrowed the custom from the Greeks and Romans, and he points to the fact that most of the inscriptions found were indeed in Greek and Latin. This opinion is probably correct because in Palestine burial was generally in a family cave, in niches, and, therefore, there was less need for identification. However, in early Mishnaic times, not all burial was in family caves. There were certainly many burials in open fields, and it was necessary to mark these accessible graves so as to keep Kohanim from blundering onto them. Therefore, as the Mishnah *Shekalim* 1:1 says, on the first of Adar each year the graves were marked. Bertinoro explains that white plaster was put on the graves, so that the priests should see them and avoid them. And since this white plaster would wear away, it was necessary to re-mark (repaint) the graves every year. Of course, this sort of marking does not mean that there were tombstones. Any mark would have been sufficient to warn off the priests.

However, there *is* a Mishnaic statement which clearly indicates the actual use of tombstones. In Mishnah *Shekalim* 2:5 we are told that if money is collected for the burial of the deceased, what is left over after the burial can be used to build a *nefesh* on his grave. This is the opinion of Nathan, but it is not the accepted law. The law is that the money left over is to be used, not for a tombstone *(nefesh)*, but for other burials. *Nefesh* means some sort of stone structure. When the same statement is quoted in the Midrash *(Genesis Rabba* 82:10), instead of *nefesh* the word *bayis* is used, which indicates that this was a houselike structure. We know, for example, that Simon the Maccabee built an elaborate structural tomb over the grave of his father and brothers (see I Maccabees 13:27 ff.). Perhaps it was in reaction against this elaborate monument that Simon ben Gamliel said *(j. Shekalim* 2:5): "We should not put up a *nefesh* [an elaborate tombstone] for the righteous; their words are their true memorial." But later commentators in defense of the tombstone said that Rabbi Simon ben Gamliel objected only to an elaborate structure, but not to a tombstone.

There certainly were tombstones in Talmudic times. The Talmud *(Horayos* 13b), mentioning the various types of action which would cause a man to forget his learning, counts in the list "reading the writing on a grave." Evidently, then, there were stones with inscriptions, but this does not prove that such an inscribed stone was *compulsory* for every grave.

The medieval authorities find justification for the use of the tombstone. Asher ben Yechiel, in his responsa 13:19, indicates that if it is customary in the family to have a tombstone, then it is to be counted among the *actual needs* of the burial. Solomon ben Aderet, in his responsa #375, says that the stone is for the honor of the dead. And in his responsa, pt. 7, #57, gives, as far as I can see, the first actual statement *mandating* a tombstone. He says that the husband is in duty bound to provide a tombstone for his wife's grave. (By the way, Greenwald, in his *Kol Bo,* top of p. 379, gives an incomplete and therefore a misleading reference. He says that the reference is Solomon ben Aderet, #57; he leaves out the necessary part, "pt. 7.")

It is on the basis of this statement of Solomon ben Aderet that the *Shulchan Aruch* gives it as a law (in *Even Hoezer* 89:1) that the husband is in duty bound to provide for the wife's burial and included in that duty is supplying a gravestone. The phrasing of Caro in the *Shulchan Aruch* would indicate that the gravestone is really an adjunct, and, in fact, this is the mood of the comment of Joel Sirkes, the *Bach,* to the *Tur, Yore Deah* 348, who says that what must be provided is "even what is not indispensable to the burial," namely, the stone.

The same offhand reference to the tombstone, implying that it is not quite essential, is in the *Shulchan Aruch, Yore Deah* 348:2, namely, "We compel the heirs of the man to provide all the needs of the father's burial and that they must include all that is in accordance with his family's custom, *even* the tombstone." So from the above it becomes clear that the tombstone is required if it happens to be the family custom to have one, but is not mandatory otherwise. The dubious status of the tombstone is finally removed by the opinion of Abraham Benjamin Sofer, the son of Moses Sofer, in his responsa *K'sav Sofer, Yore Deah* 178. He says, "Where it is customary to set up tombstones, there they are to be considered an essential part of the burial of the dead."

To sum up, as much as we can, all the above uncertainties as to the status of the tombstone, we may properly follow the opinion of Abraham Benjamin Sofer, namely, that it has now become customary in all Jewish communities to have a tombstone for the honor of the dead. The tombstone serves many purposes. One scholar (Isaac bar Sheshes, 421) says that the name is to be remembered thereby. Another, that it is an honor to the dead to come to pray there, and therefore we must know where the dead is buried. Also (as Abraham Sofer adds), if all other graves are provided with tombstones and this one grave were deprived of one, it would shame the dead who is buried there. It is for these reasons that the tombstone has become an established custom, and to the large extent to which it is true that *Minhag Yisroel Torah Hi*—i.e., that an established worthy custom of Israel is to be considered as law—we may say that in our age and in our communities, the tombstone with the name of the departed has indeed grown to be law and is mandatory.

36

COVERING THE CASKET

Nowadays many of the funerals of deceased members take place in the temple sanctuary or chapel. At these funerals the casket is sometimes of expensive bronze and at other times simpler and less expensive. A suggestion therefore has been made in the interest of equality and democracy, namely, that we should have a rule that every casket at a funeral on the temple premises should be covered with the same cloth (a pall). Is this suggestion in accordance with Jewish tradition and law? (Asked by Vigdor Kavaler, Pittsburgh, Pennsylvania.)

ANSWER:

THERE IS A long tradition in Judaism to democratize and simplify funeral procedures. The Talmud (*Ketuboth* 8b) speaks of a time when funerals had grown so expensive (especially with regard to the elaborate garments placed upon the dead) that people feared the expense, and many ran away from the task of burial of the dead in order to avoid the financial burden. Therefore Rabban Gamliel the Patriarch provided (as the Talmud put it) "simplicity for himself" *(nohag kalus)*; namely, he decided that he would be buried in a simple shroud of plain linen. Because of the example set by the patriarch, the custom then became prevalent to clothe all the dead in plain, simple linen. Also, the Talmud (*Moed Katan* 27b) describes the differences that had developed between the funeral practices of the rich and those of the poor. Among the rich, food was brought to the mourners in gold and silver bowls. Among the poor, it was brought in plain reed baskets. The rich (at the funeral meal) drank out of expensive clear glasses, the poor out of cheap colored glasses. The rich families carried out their departed in elaborate beds, while the poor carried them out in plain litters. It was ordained therefore, in order not to shame the poor, that in all these three instances the simpler practices of the poor should be followed by all. From all the above it is clear that the trend, even in the Talmudic past, was for funerals to get more and more elaborate and expensive, and therefore that efforts were constantly made to simplify them and thus democratize them. So there is no question that the inquiry made here is in harmony with an ongoing traditional sentiment.

The question asked here concentrates primarily on the matter of the casket. But in the problems and the remedies just cited in the Talmudic passage, which dealt with various examples of luxury, the litter (in our case, the casket) was only one of the problems. It is therefore necessary to consider whether the casket has indeed any special importance and what in general is its status in Jewish law and custom.

The prevalent Orthodox custom today is to use a wooden casket; even metal nails and screws are avoided, and the casket is held together by wooden pegs. One would therefore imagine that a custom now so firmly held in American Orthodox Jewish life must surely have a long history behind it. But actually that is not so. The very need

for a casket at funerals has no strong precedent in the
Jewish past. In Palestine the dead were generally wrapped
in cloths and put into the niches of the burial caves without
any casket at all. The general use of the casket developed
in Babylon, where, in the alluvial soil, no rocky caves
were available. Yet even so, when caskets did come into
use, they were not really "constructed" but were chiefly
loose boards, so the body came into direct contact with the
earth. Preferral burial was directly into the earth without a
casket (*Tur, Yore Deah* 362; also *Shulchan Aruch,* ibid.).
Complete caskets were used for Kohanim late in the six-
teenth and seventeenth centuries (cf. Joshua Falk [d. 1614]
to the *Tur,* ibid.). However, Sabbatai Cohen (*Shach,*
ibid.) says that a complete coffin may be used if earth is
placed within the casket, which would then constitute a
direct contact with earth. Clearly, then, the casket now
universally used has no special status or firm importance
in the law.

As for the material of which the casket was made (which
question is also involved here), Maimonides says it should
be of wood (*Yad, Hil. Avel,* 4:4). Nevertheless, they did
have caskets of other materials, as can be seen from the law
in *Shulchan Aruch, Yore Deah* 362:5, which states that a
coffin that has been used for one body may not be used for
another body, and it adds that if the coffin is of *stone* or
pottery, it should be broken so as not to be used again. Is,
then, the modern casket of *metal* at all permissible? This is
debated by the various authorities (see the citations in
Reform Jewish Practice, Vol. II, p. 100).

From all this it is clear that the casket is not a central or
long-established appurtenance in Jewish burial tradition.

Up to recent generations no solid casket was used. Of course, as has been mentioned, nowadays Orthodox Jews prefer a wooden casket. But it is clear that caskets of other materials were, according to many authorities, permissible. Considering that in most modern cemeteries the casket itself, when lowered into the grave, is encased in a concrete box, and therefore is far removed from direct contact with earth, then surely, as far as non-Orthodox families and congregations are concerned, there is no essential objection to a bronze casket.

However, granting that a bronze casket is, at least for us, unobjectionable, the question which is asked here still remains: Is it not against the spirit of equality and democracy that some families should use an expensive bronze casket and others a simpler, perhaps even a wooden, one? Should not all caskets be covered with a carpetlike pall to achieve the appearance of equality at funerals?

If the question of equality concerned only the casket, the matter might be much simpler. But there is a much wider difference between funerals than the type of casket used. This was always so, as the passage from *Moed Katan* 27b indicates. Nowadays, too, there are other differences between funerals than differences of the caskets. Some families have very few flowers. Others will even have a complete blanket of orchids. At the grave some families will have almost no flowers and others will have many flowers. Would we consider, then, in the interest of equality, that we ought to prohibit all flowers at our funerals or, by some rule or other, restrict the use of them? As a matter of fact, therein is one of the basic Orthodox

objections to the use of flowers at funerals. The classic
statement of the objection is made by the famous Chassidic
leader of the last generation, Eliezer Spiro (Der Muncaczer) in his responsa *Minchas Eliezer,* Vol. IV, 61. He
objects to flowers at funerals primarily because their use is
undemocratic, the rich having flowers, and the poor, few
or none at all. But in spite of such Orthodox objections to
flowers at funerals, the Chaplaincy Commission (composed of Orthodox, Conservative, and Reform rabbis)
permitted the use of flowers on Decoration Day on the
graves of Jewish soldiers. The permission is based upon
the argument that those flowers are for the honor of the
dead. Much is permitted in Jewish law in honoring the
dead.

If, therefore, it is virtually impossible to abolish or
restrict the use of flowers, which the family and friends use
to express their reverence for the dead, then by the same
token, one cannot in a modern congregation properly
prohibit any family from buying the most beautiful casket
which they feel is in honor of their dead.

This being so, what can we do to express the spirit of
equality and democracy which is a consistent and important motif in Jewish funeral history? This can still be
done, I believe, by making a distinction between what is
permanent and what is transitory, also between what is
conspicuous and what will become invisible. What is
permanent and conspicuous in the cemetery is the
tombstone. The stone stands for all to see for generations.
Many historic congregations, therefore, had committees to
supervise the choice of tombstones (and inscriptions) so
that none would be over elaborate or conspicuous (cf.

Greenwald, *Kol Bo,* p. 380). This is because of the feeling that we are all "co-partners in the cemetery" (see Moses Schick, *Yore Deah* 170).

Therefore it is important that our equality should be expressed by what is *permanently* seen in the cemetery. We need not be too much concerned by the fact that flowers may be more numerous at one funeral than another. They soon fade away. And so, too, the casket, however expensive, is buried in earth, away from view.

To sum up: Orthodox sentiment would prefer to have absolute equality in every phase of the funeral, the plain wooden casket and no flowers at all. Non-Orthodox congregations, too, should not allow too much latitude with regard to the enduring appurtenances of the cemetery, the tombstones, and the permanent planting. But with the transient and soon-to-be-invisible objects of the funeral, the established, modern, liberal custom is to allow family choice and preference. From the Orthodox point of view, there should be no casket of bronze and no flowers at all. From our point of view, these things are permissible, and we should allow a family to express itself as it wishes in this regard to honor their dead, even though one funeral may, for the brief half-hour of the service, seem more elaborate than another. After the funeral, one grave is just like another.

37

THE UNDERTAKING BUSINESS

QUESTION:

Since the burial of the dead is a commandment, a *mitzvah,*
incumbent upon every Jew, how is it permissible to have an
undertaking profession working for personal profit? On the
continent of Europe, all such work is done by the *Chevra
Kadisha,* and in England each congregation takes charge of
the burial of its members. Only in America has this *mitzvah*
become a private industry, giving profit to individuals or
companies. Is not this repugnant to the spirit of Jewish law?
(Asked by Mark King, Brooklyn, New York.)

ANSWER:

THERE IS NO doubt that the *mitzvah* of burying of the dead
was highly cherished as a religious duty and, therefore,
that in all the old Jewish communities, the organization of
men who undertook this *mitzvah*—which was called the
Chevra Kadisha, the "sacred society"—was an honored
organization to which it was a privilege to belong. The
practice with regard to funerals as it developed in England
was an outgrowth of this time-honored voluntary method
of dealing with the dead. In England each congregational
grouping has, as it were, its own burial society. Each
member of the congregation, as part of the privilege of
membership, will have the funeral needs of his family
attended to by the congregation. It therefore seems sur-

prising to the inquirer, who has lived in England, to find that in America the tasks of attending to funerals have become a business, i.e., the funeral director business, from which individuals make personal profit. Is not this situation a violation of the spirit of Jewish law, by which the community is required to perform these melancholy tasks freely as a *mitzvah*?

It will be of interest to the inquirer to know that there is one city in America in which funerals are conducted, not for private profit, but as a communal responsibility. The Sinai Memorial Chapel in San Francisco is governed by a committee composed of representatives of all shades of Jewish religious opinion and is conducted as a communal service. The chapel owns a number of cemeteries and conducts at least ninety percent of Jewish funerals in San Francisco. Whatever profits are made by the chapel are regularly distributed to institutions of Jewish education, to hospitals, and to causes in Israel. But this communal burial service is exceptional in America and is due to special historical reasons, perhaps because no Jewish undertakers came to the Pacific Coast in the early years. Other than this one exception, funeral direction in the rest of America is conducted as a regular business for profit.

This unusual fact, exceptional from the world-Jewish point of view, is due to historical reasons which explain and indeed justify the private undertaking business. The situation can best be understood by analogy with the honored institution of the rabbinate itself. The rabbinate was originally understood to be, also, a personal *mitzvah* for which there could be no pay. The Mishnah clearly states (*Bechoros* 4:6): "If a man takes pay for making a

legal decision, all his legal decisions thereby become
void." The rabbi as judge was not permitted to take pay,
nor originally was a teacher of the Torah permitted to take
pay. He was not allowed to make "worldly use of the
crown of the Torah" and "to make it a spade to dig with"
(*Ethics of the Fathers* 1:13 and 4:5). Nevertheless, by the
fourteenth century the great *mitzvah* of judging and teaching began to become a profession. This was due to
historical circumstances. The first step seems to have been
recorded by Simon ben Zemach Duran, who in 1390 was
exiled from the Spanish territories to North Africa, where
he could not make a living from his medical profession. He
therefore accepted pay for his rabbinical work. He
apologizes for this in a series of responsa (#142 to #148),
and from then on the *mitzvah* of guiding a community as a
rabbi became a profession. The chief sources discussing
this change are Joseph Caro in his *Kesev Mishnah* to the
Yad (*Hil. Talmud Torah,* Chap. 3; Moses Isserles in the
Shulchan Aruch, Yore Deah 246:21; also to *Even Hoezer*
154:21; also *Tosfos Yom Tov* (Yom Tov Lipmann Heller)
to Mishnah *Bechoros* 4:6. Then there are the responsa by
Joel Sirkes *(Bach)* 52; Meir Eisenstadt *(Panim Meiros*
I:79); Moses Sofer in his responsa *(Choshen Mishpot* 164).
In spite of this development, Obadiah Bertinoro, in his
commentary to Mishnah *Bechoros* 4:6, says he was
shocked at the rabbis in Germany, who took fees for
officiating at a divorce proceeding, and also at the witnesses, who took fees for signing the divorce document (the
Mishnah also prohibits witnesses from taking fees).

Exactly the same thing that has occurred with the
mitzvah to teach has occurred with the *mitzvah* to attend to

the dead. In Europe and in other lands, there were well-established communities with the time-honored custom of performing these sad, necessary duties through the communal committees. By the way, these committees themselves did not hesitate shrewdly to estimate the financial status of the deceased in order to know what to charge for a grave, but the funeral work itself was done as a *mitzvah* by the committee. In America individual Jews came from these historic centers. They were fragments of the larger communities of Europe. If the little synagogue established in America did have a *Chevra Kadisha,* it did not have the means to conduct the funerals, to own a cemetery, and to bury the dead. Special groups had to be organized, lodges, etc., to buy cemeteries. The little congregations could not afford it. As a result, in this new land an inevitable change took place. The funeral-directing profession and business developed to do what the tiny congregations of immigrants could not do. Therefore exactly what happened to the rabbinate centuries earlier, happened to the matter of burial here in America. It became professionalized, and as Moses Sofer said of the rabbinate in his responsa *Yore Deah* 230—that since it is a profession, the rabbi is entitled to payment for his work—so the funeral directors are entitled to pay and profit for the important communal function which history has forced upon them.

Addendum

The development of the profession and business of Jewish funeral directing is almost entirely an American

phenomenon. Since this is a definite deviation from the old
Chevra Kadisha tradition, it would be reasonable to expect
that the American Jewish Orthodox rabbinical literature
would be full of the subject. So it is rather remarkable that
there seems to be no discussion of the undertaking business
in all the responsa written by the Orthodox rabbinate, as far
as I can find. All I could discover was a passing and rather
scornful reference made by the late Rabbi Jekuthiel
Greenwald of Columbus, in his discussion of the laws of
keriah, cutting the garments (*Kol Bo* 28). He mentions
Jewish undertakers when he refers to the rather widespread
American Jewish custom of pinning a ribbon on the
garments and cutting the ribbon instead of the garments.
He calls this "a mockery, a ludicrous evasion of the law,"
which requires the mourner to cut the actual garments. In
discussing this American Jewish custom of cutting a
ribbon instead of the actual garments, he says scornfully,
"Now that the number of Jewish undertakers has increased, many violations of the law are occurring; for these
men do not listen to the instructions of the rabbis. They
make their own decisions." But even Greenwald, speaking thus angrily of those undertakers "who take the law
into their own hands," also says in a parenthesis, "but all
honor to the individuals," in other words, all honor to
those undertakers who *are* strictly Orthodox.

It is significant that in this rather denunciatory para-
graph, the rabbi objects only to the fact that many of the
undertakers are not strictly Orthodox; but he raises no
objection at all to the fact that undertakers receive pay for
performing what should be a free-will *mitzvah*. Indeed, the
very fact that no objection (as far as I can see) is found in

any other modern Orthodox responsa in America, where certainly the rabbis are in constant contact with Jewish funeral directors, indicates clearly in itself that there can be no basic objection to this professional service. In other words, it is clearly recognized by all, if only by the silence of the rabbinical scholars, that just as the rabbinate itself, due to the changes of time, ceased to be a free-will service and needed to become professional, so too the free-will duty of burying the dead had also to become professional. However, the basic religious ideal of public service still remains inherent in both professions. Thus and only thus are both professions justified in the law and ethics of Judaism.

38

THE COMPETING GENTILE UNDERTAKER

In our city there is a Jewish undertaker. His work is satisfactory. He will also bury hardship cases free of charge. He claims that the prices which he charges are just about enough to keep him solvent. But now a congregation in a neighboring town has made an arrangement with a Gentile undertaker in their own town. This undertaker charges considerably less than the Jewish undertaker in our city, who now claims that the out-of-town congregation is engaging in (or organizing) unfair competition against him. What is Jewish law and tradition on this matter that should guide our congregation in its recommendation to its members? (Asked by Rabbi Leigh D. Lerner, St. Paul, Minnesota.)

THERE IS considerable Jewish law on the matter of fair and unfair competition. In tractate *Baba Basra* 21b ff., there is the question of whether one man may open a store so close to another man's store as to hurt his business. The discussion then develops on questions of fair and unfair competition. In general these questions find the weight of the law to be against limiting competition, i.e., in favor of free trade.

But all this discussion involves competition in the same city or neighborhood. In the question asked here, we do not have competition in the same city. The competing Gentile undertaker is in another city. Nevertheless, since he attracts patrons from the larger city and away from the local Jewish undertaker, it can be considered as if he is in the same city. And so this involves the moot question of whether merchants from one city may come into another city and compete with the local merchant even if they do not locate their establishments in close proximity to the local merchants (see the references on this question given in *Modern Reform Responsa,* especially on p. 283).

But in either case the main question here is whether one merchant may cut prices to undersell another merchant. This is a matter of dispute in the Talmud, based on the Mishnah in *Baba Metzia* 4:12. Rabbi Judah forbids undercutting the price as unfair competition. But the rabbis disagree with Rabbi Judah and say that if the price is thus lowered, all the better. The law is according to the rabbis, and so it is codified in the *Shulchan Aruch, Choshen Mishpot* 228:18, and also see the end of the note by Isserles in *Choshen Mishpot* 126:5. So it is clear that according to Jewish law, the fact that one undertaker is lowering the price and hurting the business of the other undertaker is not an act forbidden by Jewish law. There are, however, other important considerations involved here.

First of all, there is the fact that the newly competing undertaker is a Gentile undertaker. If the synagogue in the smaller city had made the arrangement with a Jewish undertaker in their city, then the mere fact of the competition by undercutting of price could not in itself be objected to. But the fact that a Gentile undertaker is involved makes an important difference. It is not that Gentile undertakers may not conduct a Jewish funeral. The law specifically says (*Shulchan Aruch, Orach Chayim* 526) that if a man is to be buried on the first day of holidays, non-Jewish workers should take charge of the funeral. But what is it that Gentile workers may do? They may do the work that is forbidden to the Jews on the holiday, namely, the physical tasks of digging the grave and of making the coffin. However, washing the dead (*tahara*) and clothing the dead, that must be done by Jews (see also Greenwald, *Kol Bo*, p. 197, par. 39). Yet it must be noted that David ben Zimri in Egypt (a successor of Maimonides) permits the Gentiles to participate *with* the Jews in the washing of the body on the holiday. (Incidentally, the reference to David ben Zimri in the *Sha' are Teshuvah* is incorrect; instead of Part Two, 507, it should be Part One, 507.) Of course, if in the small town referred to there is a group of pious Jewish men and women who attend to the washing and the clothing of the body, there would be less objection to the arrangements discussed in the question. But if there is no such organization devoted to this pious task, then certainly the fact that it is a Gentile undertaker involved would be objectionable, certainly to Orthodox Jews.

There is another element besides the limitation of the functions which a Gentile undertaker may perform. It is of further importance that the established Jewish undertaker will conduct funerals free of charge in hardship cases. This is a traditional Jewish *mitzvah* that was always carried out in every community by the historic *Chevra Kadisha*. The Jewish undertaker in America, who for historical reasons has become a successor to the *Chevra Kadisha*, while indeed he is in business to make a livelihood, nevertheless he also continues the tradition of pious service and will conduct funerals in hardship cases without charge. No Gentile undertaker is under obligation to do this, nor is he likely to do this.

What, then, should be done in this complex situation? The mere fact of competition by lowering the price, especially since it is in another city, cannot, as such, be objected to. But a Jewish undertaker deserves a special status in the Jewish community. He alone, at least as far as Orthodox Jews are concerned, can carry out the intimate handling of the body, and he alone is obligated to do acts of charity, a duty which his profession inherits from the historic *Chevra Kadisha*. For that reason the community in the large city, while it cannot prohibit anybody from taking advantage of the financial benefits of the competition, nevertheless is obligated to help the Jewish undertaker as much as possible. It must also be borne in mind that the duty of burying the dead is incumbent upon every Israelite and upon every Jewish community. If, therefore, the necessity of burying hardship cases free of charge involves a cost, as it does, then the community is in duty bound to help bear that cost. In fact it does bear that cost by paying somewhat higher prices to the Jewish undertaker. This is an obligation incumbent upon the entire community. Of course, if at some time it becomes possible for the Jewish undertaker to lower his prices to meet the competition, then, as the rabbis say in *Baba Metzia*, "It is all the better." But in either case, he deserves the support of the community.

39

REBATES FROM A BUILDING FUND

QUESTION:

The congregation had a synagogue building in Philadelphia. Now it has moved to a suburb (Spring House, Pennsylvania). It sold the building in Philadelphia and used the money to buy the land for the new temple. Now a number of the contributors to the former building fund (for the Philadelphia synagogue, which was sold) are making the request that the contributions which they made for the Philadelphia synagogue be credited to them as a rebate or deduction from whatever contribution they are now asked to make for the new synagogue building. Is this request justified? (Asked by Rabbi Merle E. Singer, Beth Or Congregation, Spring House, Pennsylvania.)

ANSWER:

THE MEMBERS who are asking for this credit or rebate from the new assessment reason as follows: The money obtained by the sale of the synagogue in Philadelphia is being used to buy the land, etc., for the new synagogue. Since their contributions are part of the monies realized by the sale, their former contributions are already being used for the new building. Hence their request for credit to that amount from their new assessment. This request must be evaluated on the basis of the considerable body of law which has been built up in the tradition on the question of the building and the financing of synagogues.

168

The first thing that must be decided is this: According to Jewish law, have these members any right to make demands as to the disposal or handling of their original contributions to the synagogue in Philadelphia? To this question the answer is definitely in the negative. According to traditional law, it is only under special circumstances that a man may change the purpose or the use of a pledge to charity or to the synagogue. If a man makes a private, unvoiced mental pledge for a charitable purpose, he may without question change that pledge from one charitable purpose to another. If he has made the pledge in the presence of others, he may have to ask permission to change from one charitable cause to another. In other words, any change in the use of the money may be made as long as the money is still in his possession. However, once the money has been turned over to the officials authorized to receive it, the donor no longer has any right to make demands as to the use of the money (as long, of course, as the money has been used for the purpose to which it had been pledged). This law is based upon the Talmud *Arachin* 6b and is codified in the *Shulchan Aruch, Yore Deah* 256:6.

However, although the original donors no longer have any right to make demands with regard to their original contributions, the officers of the congregation (or the officers at the congregational meeting) have the right, if they so decide, to make decisions as to these requests by the members. But should they accede to this request?

There are a number of considerations which must guide the officers or the congregation in making a decision on this matter. The law makes a basic distinction between a synagogue in a village and a synagogue in a large city. The synagogue in a village may without question be sold outright by its members, but basically speaking, the synagogue in a large city may not be sold (*Orach Chayim* 153:7). The reason for this distinction is as follows: In a village, all the contributors or their descendants are still present, but in a large city, many visitors or traveling merchants who are no longer present may well have contributed to the building, and therefore, in a sense, the large city synagogue belongs to many absent owners and therefore may not be sold. Of course, nowadays, because of special situations in modern cities and in America, this prohibition against selling a large-city synagogue has been modified; but the basic prohibition still has weight in the law and has specific bearing on our question, namely, that there are certainly many former members of the congregation in Philadelphia who did *not* move to the suburb. If credit for former contributions be given to those members who *have* moved to the suburb, then those who have not moved to the suburb have equal rights to the property of the synagogue. They too, therefore, may now demand to be credited with their former contributions and perhaps ask that their gift be now transferred to some other congregation to which they at present belong. Thus, giving credit for a former contribution to a metropolitan synagogue could easily become a dangerous precedent.

Aside from the fact that giving credit to former members could create a bad precedent, there is also a more definite traditional law involved here, namely, the law governing the proper use of monies obtained from the sale of a synagogue building. With regard to the use of this sale money, the law is clearly stated in the *Tur* and *Shulchan Aruch* #193 based upon Mishnah *Megillah* 3:1. It is as follows: The money realized from the sale of the synagogue is considered to be sacred money and may not be used for any purpose less sacred than that which has been sold. Thus, for example, the Ark is more sacred than the rest of the building. A Sefer Torah is more sacred than the Ark, etc. The monies obtained from the sale of such objects share the sacredness of the object which has been sold. The monies, therefore, obtained from the sale of a synagogue building may be used for another synagogue building, which is equally sacred, or for an Ark, which is still more holy. But the money may not be used for anything less holy (see especially 153:5). Thus in this case the money obtained from the sale of the Philadelphia synagogue may not be used for the reimbursement of private individuals. This would be a drastic misuse of sacred money. In other words, although the money will be used for another synagogue, since it will also be a rebate to these individuals, it is in effect being used for private benefit, since it leaves them with less to pay out on the new assessment.

There is also another practical consideration involved. If these members get their former gifts deducted from the present assessment, there will, of course, be less money available for the building of the new temple. This fact might well create a greater burden upon all the other members. This fact involves the law of how the money for a new synagogue must be assessed. There are different modes of assessment established in the legal tradition for different types of synagogue expenses. If, for example, there is a need to hire a cantor for the holidays, the cost for this may be met by an equal assessment imposed upon every individual member. But a capital expense, such as the building of a synagogue, is not met by an equal per capita assessment but by special assessments made according to the financial ability of the various members. This law is stated clearly by Meir of Padua in his responsa #42 and is referred to in the *Be' er Hetev* to *Orach Chayim* 150. Now we must assume that the original contributors to the older temple could afford to have given those contributions and now can still afford to make a larger (and not a smaller) contribution to the new temple. Of course, the former contributors who are making the present demand for credit may claim that to demand a second large contribution to the synagogue constitutes excessive pressure put upon them even though they can afford it. But the law clearly states that when it comes to the high purpose of building a synagogue, members of the community may exert the necessary pressure on each other (*"kofin zeh es zeh," Tur* and *Shulchan Aruch, Orach Chayim* 150).

To sum up: The donors to the old synagogue no longer have any right to make demands as to the disposal or handling of their former gifts, since those gifts had already come into the hands of the authorized officers. The authorized officers of the congregation (alone or at a congregational meeting) have the right to make all such decisions. The officers must now consider the fact that in a large-city congregation, many people not now living in the new location also have certain rights in the old synagogue property. They must also consider that it is clearly against traditional law for them to convert part of the purchase money into what amounts to private funds. They must decide now how much may be justly assessed. This decision must not be based upon past gifts, but on the present needs of the building fund and the ability of the prospective donors to meet the assessment.

As for the donors involved, once the traditional laws are put before them, they are not likely to press their demands for what amounts to a rebate. They have already earned spiritual credit for their contributions to the Philadelphia synagogue. They will surely not insist also on a financial credit for a past *mitzvah* which they had properly and generously fulfilled.

Addendum

There has developed in American congregations a method of raising building-fund money which differs from the traditional method of asking members to pay according to their ability. The newer method, followed in a number of congregations, is to assess all members equally as an addition to their membership dues, with allowance made, of course, for hardship cases. Suppose, then, in the case mentioned in the responsum, that members of the congregation were taxed for the original building fund and now claim it is unjust to be taxed a full amount again for the second building fund. Is not the situation different from what is described in the above responsum? This may well depend upon what the plan was when the original synagogue building was acquired. If, for example, the original building was meant to be permanently the synagogue of the congregation, and if it was used as such, let us say, for ten years, then it is a complete building enterprise in itself, and the money contributed to it can be deemed sacred money and none of it can be used for the lesser sanctity of helping the financial burden of individual members.

If, however, it was understood when the original building was acquired that this was perhaps temporary and therefore the gifts given to it were given with the condition or understanding that it was part of some future enterprise, when a more permanent suburban synagogue would be built, then both building enterprises are really one and the gifts or assessments given for one are also given for this new building, and therefore if any individual wishes some adjustment, he may ask for it and be granted it.

40

TEMPLE MEMBERSHIP AND CHARITY

QUESTION:

Our congregation has a bylaw that one of the conditions of membership is an annual contribution to the United Jewish Fund. One family in the congregation objects to this bylaw as a coercion of conscience. What would be the attitude of Jewish tradition to this bylaw of our congregation? (Asked by Rabbi Wolli Kaelter, Long Beach, California.)

ANSWER:

THERE ARE A number of social clubs in the various Jewish communities of America which will not accept a person into their membership unless he is a contributor to the United Jewish Fund. However, I am not at the moment aware of any congregation that has this requirement. The fact that I do not know of any such congregation would indicate that such a requirement is not likely to be a widespread practice, but this does not mean, necessarily, that a congregation is wrong if it *does* have this rule. Besides, it is not only a question of this congregation alone; there may well be other congregations that already have such a requirement and, also, it may be that situation will change and other congregations may wish to add such a requirement. For these reasons, it is important that the question raised here by the Long Beach congregation be discussed basically on the grounds of Jewish law and tradition. What, then, is the attitude of Judaism to the giving of charity, specifically to the charities of the organized community, and what relation does this giving of charity have to the Jewish religion itself and to the congregation?

The giving of charity is a *mitzvah* of special status. It is one of those *mitzvos* which have a double mandate. It is both a positive commandment and a negative commandment. As a positive commandment, it is Number 480 in the list and is based upon the verse in Deuteronomy 15:8: "Thou shalt open thy hand to the needy." And as a negative commandment it is Number 479 and is based upon Deuteronomy 15:7: "Do not close thy hand" (i.e., from giving). Since it is a *mitzvah* of double status, it is therefore incumbent upon *everyone*. Hence even a poor man who is himself a recipient of charity must give charity too as his religious duty (*Yore Deah* 248:1, based upon *Gittin* 7b, top). As one gives charity, he must give it joyously; in other words, not show any ill-tempered reluctance (*Yore Deah* 249:3).

Furthermore, the spiritual status of charity, besides its status of a commandment, positive and negative, is that the promise to give charity has the religious status of a sacred vow (*Yore Deah* 255b). For all these reasons, because it is a positive and a negative commandment, and because it has the sacred status of a vow, Maimonides says one must be more careful in the fulfillment of the duty of charity than with any other of the positive commandments (*Yad, Matnas Aniim* 10:1).

Therefore, it is not surprising that the giving of charity is one of those few commandments of which the law says that we may exercise social pressure to insure its fulfillment. One other such commandment is the building of a synagogue. The members of a community may bring pressure on each other to organize and maintain a synagogue (*Orach Chayim* 150) and, according to some opinions, may exercise compulsion to see that there is a *minyan* always; that is to say, if there are only ten people, one may not leave the city without providing a substitute (*Orach Chayim* 55:22). So, in a similar way, the codes indicate that the same type of communal pressure *(kofin zeh es zeh)* must be brought to bear to see that the commandment to give charity is fulfilled. This is based upon the Talmud in *Kesuvos* 49b. The *Tosfos* raises some objection to this compulsion and then justifies it, and it is further justified by David ben Zimri in his commentary to Maimonides (ibid. 7:10).

If this is the case, as it manifestly is, that charity is so vital and inescapable a *religious* duty, then why is it that not every synagogue in America has this requirement? The answer, of course, lies in the difference between the organization of Jewish communities in America and the Old World. In the Old World the community was one organization, even though there may have been many synagogues; and in many of the European communities the amount of charity to be given was actually apportioned, just as the taxes were (see the *Tosfos* to *Gittin* 7b quoted above). But in America, where the Jewish communities were built up slowly from fragments of various and differing Jewish communities, each congregation became a separate and independent unit. This fact, by the way,

created considerable changes in Jewish law as to the right
to sell a synagogue, etc. So in America the organization of
charities became community-wide independently, but was
separate from the synagogue. Why, then, did not the
various synagogues demand an active role in the charity
organizations, since charity was a *religious* duty? The
answer was a practical one. There developed a sort of
division of function, especially in the large communities.
Some individuals became active in the charities, and
others became active in the synagogues. Besides, the
charities organized great propaganda pressure for contributions and considerable publicity annually, which
made it unnecessary for the synagogue to participate as an
organization.

However, in a smaller community, where there is
limited activist manpower, those active in maintaining the
synagogue are to a considerable extent the same as those
maintaining the communal charities, and it is natural for
them to want both types of organizations to help each
other.

If they do so, as they have done in the Long Beach
congregation, they are fully in accord with Jewish religious tradition, which considers charity a *spiritual* obligation upon every Jew, whatever his financial status. And,
also, tradition gives the right to a congregation or community to exercise social pressure *(kofin)* to guarantee the
fulfillment of this commandment.

41

A SURVIVOR'S SENSE OF GUILT

QUESTION:

A survivor of a concentration camp is under psychiatric care because of a deep sense of guilt. He and his wife were together in camp, and she became pregnant by him. Then the Nazis issued an order that all pregnant women be killed. Now the man feels that he was guilty of the death of his wife. What help can be given to the psychiatrist from the point of view of Jewish law? (Asked by Sonia Syme, Detroit, Michigan.)

ANSWER:

WHATEVER MISFORTUNE occurs to one dear to us, it is almost a natural impulse for us to feel guilty. We think that if we had only done something different or said something different, the misfortune to our dear one might never have occurred. In this manner, decent, kindly people embitter their own lives. The question here is, how can this husband, who survived while his wife was killed by the Nazis, emerge from this cloud of self-assumed guilt?

A person under this load of guilt must seek for a rational refutation of this pathetic emotion. If he is guilty because his wife was killed, who should be guilty for all the Jewish children who were led to the slaughter? If the parents of these murdered innocents are alive, should they feel that if they only had not had these children, the children would not have suffered? Or should the parents of the many adults who were killed, if any of those old people are alive, feel guilty that they produced these lambs for the slaughter? Such a pathetic sense of guilt of a parent generation for having brought children into a world of misery, or a sense of guilt imputed by the children to these parents for having brought the unhappy children into the world, is quite natural and, in fact, is found a number of times in Scripture. Job in Chapter 3 curses the day in which he was born and that his mother brought forth a man-child destined for misery. And also the Prophet Jeremiah (15:10) complains retroactively, as it were, "Woe that my mother bore me to be a man of misery and strife." These emotional feelings of guilt or imputations of guilt are a natural reaction, although of course illogical, for how could parents know beforehand what might be the fate of the children?

So in this case, too, this couple did not know beforehand of the decree that pregnant women would be killed. Of course, had they known of this decree beforehand, and nevertheless ran the risk of pregnancy knowing that it would mean death, then some sense of guilt would be understandable and even justified. The case would then be like that of a wife whose life is endangered if she becomes pregnant. In that case, Moses Feinstein, the great Orthodox authority of our day (*Igros Moshe, Even Hoezer* 13), decided that the couple should either refrain from sexual intercourse or use available contraceptive devices. But this is not the case here. The couple did not know beforehand of the murderous Nazi decree. It came afterwards.

Since the intercourse occurred between husband and wife before there was knowledge of any danger to life, then the very act of intercourse deserves praise. If in the very shadow of death for both of them in the concentration camp, they wanted to produce children, this indicates a blessed and noble sense of hope that there would yet be a future and a generation of Jewish children who could live happily.

Aside from their implied hopefulness, it must also be stated that from the point of view of strict Jewish law, the bearing of children is deemed to be a supreme *mitzvah,* a God-given mandate. In fact, the Talmud (*Yevamos* 63b) and *Shulchan Aruch* (*Even Hoezer* 1:1) say that he who refrains from the effort to produce children is as if he himself is a shedder of blood (i.e., he destroys the future). The verse upon which this Talmudic decision is based is of singular appropriateness to this special situation. It is based on the words that God spoke to Noah and his family when they emerged from the Ark. The verse in Genesis 9:7 says, "Be ye fruitful and multiply," and the preceding verse to which this is appended is, "He that sheds a man's blood, by man shall his blood be shed." In other words, precisely because there is murder and genocide in the world, it is a man's mandate to participate in the preservation of the species.

We may say that Genesis 9:6 can refer to the murderous Nazis, and verse 7 refers to such as he and his wife. So let him not take on himself the guilt of the shedders of blood. What he did was his religious duty and a vote of hope in the human race and its future.

42

WEDDING BEFORE THE OPEN ARK

QUESTION:

A couple about to be married in the synagogue asked that during the ceremony the doors of the Ark be opened. Should this request be granted? (Asked by Vigdor Kavaler, Pittsburgh, Pennsylvania.)

ANSWER:

NOWADAYS MANY young couples about to be married feel very independent-minded about the wedding service. They seem to be of the opinion that since it is *their* wedding, they have the right to dictate, to a considerable degree, the form of the ceremony. In these days of increased mixed marriages, rabbis are naturally inclined to be concessive to the requests of any couple that wishes to be married by a rabbi. Of course, some of these special requests are of no important consequence and can be granted readily, but some are of such a nature that they cannot be granted at all. Some couples will ask that the rabbi officiate with a Christian minister. This will, of course, occur in mixed marriages, not when both groom and bride are Jews. Some couples seem to wish to write the entire service themselves. Other couples insist upon having certain poetry or certain loving paragraphs that they have written to each other included in the traditional ceremony. This limited request is generally granted because it does not involve any omission of the traditional essentials of the service but is merely an addition which is of no special consequence.

But a request has come recently that during the wedding ceremony the doors of the Holy Ark be open so that the Torahs be visible. Should this request be among those which the rabbi can readily grant?

It is necessary, first of all, to make clear the Halachic status of our present custom, in all Reform and most Conservative congregations (and now in some Orthodox congregations), to have the wedding ceremony in the synagogue auditorium itself. This is an important and a controversial question. Large sections of Jewry, primarily Orthodox, consider it quite wrong to hold the ceremony indoors. I have been informed that in certain Chassidic marriages in New York, when the marriage takes place in a hired hall, the ceremony is conducted under an open skylight. The preference for marriages to take place in the open air is based upon a statement by Moses Isserles in *Shulchan Aruch, Even Hoezer* 61:1, in which he says, "Some say that a marriage should take place under the open sky as a good omen [*simmon tov*] to symbolize God's blessing to Abraham that his descendants shall be as numerous as the stars of the heaven." Moses Sofer, the great Hungarian authority, in his responsa *(Even Hoezer* 98) insists that this suggestion of Isserles be strictly followed, and he says, further, that those who do not follow it are merely imitating the Christian custom of having marriages in the church.

However, in spite of the suggestion of Isserles and the

insistence of Moses Sofer, it cannot be said that it is an actual law that the marriage must take place out of doors. As a matter of fact, Maharil, the great Rhenish authority (especially in the field of our Ashkenazic *minhagim),* always conducted marriages within the synagogue. There was indeed a preliminary ritual outside of the synagogue in the courtyard, but the marriage itself, with the blessings, took place in the synagogue itself (Maharil, *Hil. Chasuna).*

An interesting modern discussion as to whether marriages may or may not take place in the synagogue is found in the responsa of the modern Orthodox authority, Moses Feinstein *(Even Hoezer* #93). He was asked the following question: A rabbi of an Orthodox congregation was required by the congregation to attend (if not to participate in) all the marriages of the congregation members. In this Orthodox congregation, the marriages take place in the synagogue. Therefore this rabbi asks Moses Feinstein whether, because of the statements of Isserles and Moses Sofer, he should refuse to attend the weddings in the synagogue even though, if he does refuse to attend, he may lose his position. Moses Feinstein (while he did not quote the actual practice of Maharil, who conducted marriages in the synagogue) says that Isserles' statement is not law—it is only good advice for a good omen *(simmon tov)* for those who wish to follow it; and as for the prohibition against synagogue marriages by Moses Sofer, that was stated under special circumstances. Moses Sofer was fighting the custom of the Reformers, whom he accused of imitating the practices of Gentile church weddings by having the weddings in the synagogue. But actually, says Moses

Feinstein, the rabbi may attend the marriages in the synagogue, and in fact, he is in duty bound to attend to see that they are conducted according to Jewish law. So it is clear that our present general custom of having the marriages in the synagogue, while contrary to the rather widespread practice of having them in the open air, is nevertheless fully in accord with Jewish legal tradition.

However, there is one significant difference between Reform marriages in the synagogue and Orthodox marriages besides, of course, the variations in ritual. The difference relevant to our discussion is the location *within* the synagogue where the wedding takes place.

When Maharil conducted the wedding ceremony in the synagogue in Mainz, the ceremony took place on the *bimah* (he calls it *migdal*), i.e., the reading desk and enclosure which, in all Orthodox synagogues, is in the center of the synagogue, about equidistant between the Ark and the exit doors. So today in Orthodox synagogues, when the ceremony does take place in the synagogue, it likewise takes place upon the *bimah*, the reading enclosure in the center of the synagogue. But in Reform congregations and in most Conservative congregations, the *bimah*, the center of the synagogue, has long since been omitted. The seating now is solid from the Ark to the door. Therefore, when marriages take place in a Reform or Conservative congregation, they take place on the platform right in front of and close to the Ark. Thus these marriages already are in the most sacred part of the synagogue, which is not at all inappropriate since marriage is a sacred institution and the ceremony is called *Kiddushin*, "sacredness." The Ark, too, is considered *tashmishey kedusha,* "the appurtenances of the holy," so it is quite appropriate that the wedding ceremony, called *Kiddushin,* should take place right in front of the Ark, which is *tashmishey kedusha.*

Even when the Ark is closed, it must be understood that the precinct is considered sacred. If so, then why may a preacher stand with his back to the Ark during the sermon? The answer given is that when the Ark doors are closed, the Ark is considered a separate enclosure. Besides, the preacher stands there for only a limited time. It would be considered wrong, however, for people so to be seated in the synagogue that their backs are toward the closed Ark. In fact, those pious people who would spend a whole night of Yom Kippur in the synagogue are expected to be very careful that when they fall asleep, they are seated as far as possible from the Ark. It is even said that when people leave the synagogue, they should not turn their backs completely on the Ark, but rather sidle out through the door. (All the above laws and customs are described in the *Encyclopedia Talmudit* under the heading *"Aron Ha-Kodesh."*) So it is clear that even when the Ark is closed, we must be aware and considerate of its sanctity. Nevertheless, for the brief time of the wedding ceremony, it is permissible that the rabbi or the married couple will have their backs toward the Ark, since the closed Ark is considered a separate enclosure.

But now comes the additional request—which seems to be based on the feeling that the sanctity of the closed Ark is insufficient—that the doors of the Ark be opened and the sacred scrolls be visible to all during the wedding ceremony.

This suggestion raises certain difficulties, if not in law, at least in custom. Many authorities and many communities insist that whenever the Ark is open, the congregation must stand. Therefore, during the service on Sabbath and holidays, when the Torah is taken out to be read, all communities follow the rule that people stand while the Torah is moved from the Ark to the reading desk; but some communities will stand as long as the Ark is open (see the authorities cited in *Contemporary Reform Responsa,* pp. 37–39). Therefore, the custom has developed in some communities, for the sake of the congregation, not to keep the Ark open after the Torahs are taken out. Therefore, keeping the Ark open during a wedding ceremony might lead many to feel that the sacredness of the visible Sefer Torahs would require them to stand all through the wedding ceremony, which would certainly be a hardship for many.

Furthermore, on certain special occasions of worship, such as Yom Kippur, the Ark doors are solemnly opened. Is it wise, then, to destroy the uniqueness and the special impressiveness of those worship occasions by making the open Ark a frequent and, therefore, commonplace event?

To sum up, it cannot be said that there is a definite law against having the doors of the Ark open during a wedding ceremony, but sentiment and general good sense would be opposed to such a practice. If a couple insists on it, and if the circumstances are such that it is better to give in to their request, that may be done. But, in general, there is a danger that if it is permitted for one couple, others will deem it a privilege which they are entitled to also, and soon it would become common practice. It is this danger that must be avoided. Let the couple understand that having their ceremony on the platform right by the Holy Ark is certainly sacredness enough, and the request to open the Ark should, for the sake of the convenience of the congregation and retaining the solemnity of the special religious services, be discouraged as much as possible.

43

APOSTATE WEDDING ATTENDANTS

QUESTION:

The sister of the bride has converted to Christianity. Now this convert wishes to stand under the *chuppah* as an attendant at her sister's wedding. Should this be permitted? (Asked by Rabbi David Polish, Chicago, Illinois.)

ANSWER:

IT IS NECESSARY, first, to consider the actual status in Jewish law of the apostate from Judaism. Then, after considering the legal status of the apostate, we must come to a conclusion suitable to our present circumstances as to the rights of this apostate in the wedding ceremony of her sister.

In Deuteronomy 22:1–3, Scripture speaks of strayed cattle and other lost objects. It declares it to be the duty of everyone to protect these strayed or lost objects until the owner can search them out and recover them. In verse 3, Scripture says: "Thus shall you do with regard to all things lost by thy brother." R. Jochanan, in *Avoda Zara* 26b, says, "I take the Scriptural word 'brother' to include the apostate." Also, the phrase in *Sanhedrin* 44a, "Although he has sinned, he is still an Israelite," applies as a general principle to the apostate. Note that *Pachad Yitzchok* (s.v. *Mumar)* applies this phrase a number of times to the apostate. Of course the law makes a distinction between a hostile apostate *(mumar l'hachis)* and an apostate merely out of supposed self-benefit or self-gratification *(mumar l'teovone)*. These two different groups are met, of course, with different attitudes, but legally they are Jews, *poshey Yisroel,* sinful Jews, but still Jews.

These general maxims which include the apostate in the Jewish fold are exemplified and emphasized by the fact that certain vital Jewish functions, if performed by an apostate, are fully valid. This rule applies especially in matters of family life. If a woman's husband has become an apostate, her marriage cannot be dissolved unless her apostate-husband gives her a *get.* In this divorce document the apostate may not use his new Gentile name but must use his old Jewish name, since it is still his name *(Even Hoezer* 129:5). If a man dies childless, his wife must get *chalitza* before she can marry again. She must get the *chalitza* from her husband's brother even if the brother is now an apostate *(Even Hoezer* 157:4). (There are some variations of this law, but they do not directly concern us here.) This unbroken kinship with the apostate is to be seen also in the laws of inheritance. An apostate is entitled to inherit his father's estate; and if he is the first-born, he still has the additional rights of a first-born *(Choshen Mishpot* 283:2).

Now if an apostate can validly perform and participate in these vital legal situations, there certainly can be no legal objection to an apostate being an attendant at a wedding. The wedding attendant is not an indispensable functionary. A Jewish wedding is legal if the husband proposes to the wife and gives her an object of value, and she accepts it in the presence of witnesses. Here the apostate sister is not necessary as a witness. There are other witnesses present, and so there can be no legal objection to her participating in the wedding.

This is the purely legal situation. But in all relationships with an apostate, there is, of course, some natural human reaction. We have suffered so cruelly through the centuries from the slanders and machinations of apostates that their very presence becomes hard for a Jew who knows Jewish history to endure. Of course, those bitter enemies of ours were *mumar l' hachis*. While it is reasonable to assume that this girl has no hostile intention at all, but has converted out of convenience, she is a *mumar l' teovone*. Nevertheless, to the extent that we are guided by our Jewish feelings, any sort of *mumar* is objectionable.

Thus it is that although the law gives a *mumar* virtually every legal right, the law still expresses caution in dealing with them. For example, in the laws of *shechitah* (*Yore Deah* 2:2, 4), as a general rule the apostate's *shechitah* is kosher, but he must be carefully examined and watched. In the laws of inheritance, while the apostate may legally inherit, the rabbis under certain circumstances have stopped the transfer of property from a Jew to an apostate (see *Choshen Mishpot* 283:2). In other words, we judge the special circumstances before we decide whether or not we permit an apostate to exercise his privileges in Judaism, although it is legal for him to do so.

Thus in this case, the rabbi by tradition has leeway to go by his personal judgment. He must consider the communal and also the family situation. If having the apostate sister stand under the *chuppah* next to the bride at the marriage

will be taken by many in the community as a condoning of
apostasy and may, therefore, tend to increase such occurrences, then the rabbi has the right *l' migdor milso,* to make
"a fence of protection" and forbid the apostate's participation. If, however, there is no danger of misunderstand-
ing, then we must remember the legal status of the apostate
in general. Nevertheless it would be wise not to have her
there if it is a very small wedding. If there are more people
present who are considered the legal witnesses, and if there
is no danger of her presence being taken as condoning
apostasy, then there can be no legal objection to her
presence. Furthermore, one must also consider the family
situation. If the parents of the bride are eager to have their
daughter present, and if the bride herself is eager to have
her sister, then forbidding her to participate could easily do
more harm than good, especially since, after all, there is no
real legal objection to her presence.

44

REMARRIAGE OF RUSSIAN IMMIGRANTS

QUESTION:

Almost all of the married Russian immigrants nowadays were married in the Soviet-style civil ceremony. An Orthodox colleague suggested that the immigrant couples should be remarried with Jewish marriage. Is this necessary? (Asked by Rabbi Richard A. Zionts, Shreveport, Louisiana.)

ANSWER:

SADLY ENOUGH, this is not a new question. It came up frequently and grievously after the fifteenth century, when Marranos kept escaping from Spain and Portugal into Jewish communities. These Marranos had been married as ostensible Christians in the church by a priest.

When they escaped, the question of the Jewish legitimacy of their marriages came up in a tragic form. Generally Marrano couples did not escape together and by the same route. For safety's sake they escaped separately by different routes. So it would happen that a wife would safely reach a Jewish community and the husband would be lost and never appear. The woman, then, was an *agunah* and could never marry anyone else.

There was a strong humane tendency on the part of the rabbinate to declare the Marrano church marriages null and void so that the woman need not remain an *agunah*. The classic responsum on this matter, and in the circumstances just outlined above, was by Isaac bar Sheshes in Algiers, in his responsum #6. On the basis of this responsum, Joseph Caro, in the *Shulchan Aruch, Even Hoezer* 149:6, says that the marriage of two apostates has no Jewish validity, and Isserles to *Even Hoezer* 26:1 makes virtually the same decision. However, even in the early decisions with regard to the Marranos, there were some doubts as to this negative decision. It might have been, for example, that before going to church, the Marrano couple had met privately and a ring was given and the proper words were recited. Also, if there were Jewish witnesses present, that too would count toward making the marriage Jewishly valid.

It is relevant to the present question that Isaac bar Sheshes, whose responsum is the source of the decision that the Marrano church marriage had no Jewish validity, gives two main reasons for his opinion. First, the couple made no attempt to have some sort of Jewish marriage but seemed completely content with the church marriage; hence, he said, it is clear that it was not their intention to have marriage in the Jewish sense *kiddushin*. Second, there were no witnesses to the fact that the couple lived together as man and wife. Had there been such Jewish witnesses, he says, then the marriage could have been considered valid on that basis alone *(ayday yichud)*.

Applying these two arguments to the situation of the Russian immigrants, we must say, first of all, that we do not know that they were quite content with the Soviet-style civil marriage. It well may be that they would have preferred to have a Jewish religious type of marriage. This preference has bearing on the Jewish validity of their marriage because it would indicate an *intention* that the relationship should be truly a marriage, and such an intention counts toward according the relationship Jewish validity. Secondly, it well may be that even if they were married only in the Soviet registry office, they lived together in the presence of other Jews as man and wife. That fact, too, would tend to give Jewish validity to their marriage.

In modern times this question has come up very frequently. There are no Marranos forced into another religion to save their lives, but there is a widespread availability in the western lands of civil marriage. Very many Jews are married by a judge or a justice of the peace. The old question, therefore, comes up again. Are these civil marriages, which are without Jewish religious ritual, to be considered valid marriages by the Jewish religion? The reason for the widespread discussion of this question is basically the same as it was with the Marranos. It is a question of Jewish divorce, the *get*. If, as often happens, an ex-husband is no longer available to give a *get*, the woman remains an *agunah* and cannot remarry Jewishly.

Therefore, there is a tendency among some authorities to find ways of considering the civil marriage invalid Jewishly so that the woman may not need a *get* and so can remarry. But since civil marriages are now widespread, it is an extremely delicate matter to declare the marriages of tens of thousands of Jews invalid. Therefore, there is uncertainty among the scholars.

The well-known authority Joseph Henkin, in his *Prushey Ibra,* accepts the validity of civil marriages. After all, a ring is exchanged, words of marriage are spoken, and

generally the couple lives in a Jewish community, where
they are known as man and wife. The one authority who is
inclined to invalidate civil marriages is Moses Feinstein,
but he is always strict. In the case of the unavailability of a
get, he declared marriages by a Reform rabbi null and
void. So it is not surprising that for the sake of an *agunah*
and in general, he would consider non-Orthodox weddings
invalid. However, he is aware that the subject is debatable,
as can be seen by the very fact of how often he discusses it
in the various volumes of *Igros Moshe.* And even he, strict
as he is, will admit the validity of a civil marriage under
certain special circumstances which have direct bearing on
the question asked. In his responsum #75, he speaks of a
couple who married in court but have frequently lived
together in a Jewish environment, so there are "kosher"
Jewish witnesses who know them as man and wife. This
would make the marriage valid. So he concludes that such
marriage is valid enough to require a *get,* though he would
be willing to invalidate even this marriage in order to
rescue an *agunah.*

Now directly as to the Russian immigrants, they are not
apostates to another religion, whose marriages Joseph
Caro and Isserles would declare invalid. They were simply
required to go through civil marriage. It was not their
choice. They considered this a marriage, and they meant it
to be valid marriage, not an adulterous relationship.
Furthermore, if at that civil marriage, the man gave the
woman a ring and said words indicating marriage, that
fulfills the need for Jewish marriage, which requires "he
must give and he must say . . ." Besides, there may well
have been Jewish witnesses at the ceremony, and

moreover, most of them lived in a Jewish community, and there certainly may have been secretly observing Jews there, who knew them as married. All this is enough to make their marriage valid as Jewish marriage.

To require them to be remarried is to tell them thereby that the Jewish community which now welcomes them, considers that they have been living together without legal marriage. Such an attitude would be completely unjustified in light of the reasons given above for accepting their marriage as Jewishly valid.

Furthermore, we have now, in every modern Jewish community, a considerable number of couples who have been united only by civil marriage just as the Russian immigrants have. Will we undertake to say that all of these also are not living in valid marriage? Of course, if any of the Russian immigrants, of their own accord, were to ask for a Jewish ceremony, that might be allowed them, but even in this regard, we should hesitate because it would imply that they were not validly married hitherto. We might conduct such an occasional religious marriage, but certainly not require it as essential.

45

REMARRIAGE OF A WIDOWER

QUESTION:

According to the Halachah, how soon may a widower remarry? (Asked by Rabbi Roland Gittelsohn, Boston, Massachusetts.)

ANSWER:

THE SOURCE of the law is the Talmud (*Moed Katan* 23a), where it is stated that a widower may not remarry until the three festivals (Passover, Shavuos, Succos) have passed. In other words, he must wait virtually a whole year. The reason for this rather long delay in the permission to remarry is given by the *Tosfos* to the passage in *Moed Katan*. The man should be given time for thoughts of his first wife to fade from his memory. He should not marry one woman while his heart is still full of memories of another woman. The *Tosfos* uses the frequently employed phrase: that there should not be two different moods in the same bed, *"shtay dayos b'mito."* Asher ben Yechiel, in his notes to the Talmud passage, refers to the same emotional problem in a somewhat different way. He cites the opinion that if the widower will have the joy of the three happy festivals without his deceased wife by his side, she will then tend to fade from his mind.

The passage in the Talmud referred to above adds the

following—if the widower has not fulfilled the duty of having children (which means at least a son and a daughter) or if his deceased wife left him with little children who need to be taken care of, then he may remarry at once. In this case, "at once" means he may have the marriage ceremony after the seven days have ended, but he must wait until after the thirty days of mourning before they have conjugal relations.

This law as stated in the Talmud is given in almost the identical words in the *Shulchan Aruch, Yore Deah* 392:2. However there Isserles adds that the custom has developed that the widower may remarry earlier than the passing of three festivals. This statement of Isserles, that the custom has developed that the widower need not wait for the passing of the three festivals, indicates that the custom must have been based on the opinion of various earlier scholars who sought to bring about a relaxation of the three-festival requirement. So it has been indeed. For example, the post-Talmudic treatise on mourning, *Semachos* (7:15), repeats the Talmudic relaxation that if there are no children, or if he has only small children, the widower may remarry at once, i.e., after thirty days. The *Shach* (Sifse Cohen) to the *Shulchan Aruch* cites the early Halachic booklet *Aguda* to the effect that Yom Kippur and Rosh Hashonah may be counted as two of the festivals. This would, of course, greatly reduce the time of waiting. For example, if the wife died before Rosh Hashonah and Yom Kippur, the widower could remarry immediately after Succos. Also, Ezekiel Landau, in his *Shulchan Aruch* commentary *Dagul Mirvovo,* says that one may count Shemini Atzeres as a festival for this purpose. Another of the many indications of a steady tendency toward leniency is the opinion of Jekuthiel Teitelbaum in his *Avne Zedek* (*Even Hoezer* #18). He speaks of a young widower who was hesitant about remarrying before the three festivals had passed. His father, however, wanted him to remarry sooner. In that case, Teitelbaum decided that the duty of "honor thy father" supersedes the duty of the three festivals and he should obey his father and marry sooner.

Asher ben Yechiel, in his commentary to the Talmud passage, cites an additional personal reason why the widower need not wait. It is not only if he has had no children or if he has small children that need to be taken care of, but also if he has no one to take care of him. Asher ben Yechiel gets this from the Yerushalmi, *Yevamos* 4:6b. The post-Talmudic book *Semachos* adds an incident from the life of Rabbi Tarfon (this is also taken from the Yerushalmi, ibid.). The Babylonian Talmud in *Moed Katan* 23a gives the same anecdote as happening to Joseph the Priest. Rabbi Tarfon, as soon as his wife died, said to his wife's sister, "Come and take care of your sister's little children," which was a proposal of marriage to her, but they did not have conjugal relations until thirty days had passed. The Babylonian Talmud, reporting this same incident about Joseph the Priest, said that he actually made his proposal to his wife's sister at the cemetery. All of which, in essence, sums up the clearly permissive tendency of the law.

There are, however, some cautionary opinions also. Moses Sofer in his responsa (*Yore Deah* 351) says that if the deceased wife's sister is to be the widower's second wife, he must not have the wedding ceremony within the thirty days (a ceremony which would be permitted if he had no children) because she also is in mourning for his first wife, who was her sister. Also, Baruch Teomim Frankel, in his commentary *Imre Baruch* to the *Shulchan Aruch*, says that if the marriage is as early as a month after the bereavement, there should be a minimum of dancing and festivities.

Yet for all these cautionary statements, one may say that the Halachah, as it has developed, has managed virtually to abolish the three-festival requirement, either because of the man's need to take care of his children, etc., or by counting in other festivals besides the three main ones in order to shorten the waiting period. As Isserles indicates, the custom of early marriage has virtually abolished the law of the three-festival wait. But Isserles adds that a sensitive man should perhaps be hesitant in this matter.

46

INSEMINATION WITH MIXED SEED

QUESTION:

> At a discussion on the question of artificial insemination, a physician said that if she (the physician) finds that the sperm of the husband is not potent enough (a low sperm count), she requests that the brother and the father of her patient's husband bring in their sperm. The three sperm are mixed and injected in the wife. Would this be permitted in Jewish law? (Asked by Sonia Syme, Detroit, Michigan.)

ANSWER:

THE QUESTION of artificial insemination has already been discussed in the *Conference Yearbook,* Vol. 62, 1953, and in *Reform Responsa,* pp. 212 and 217. Since then the whole question has received increasing attention from Halachic authorities, the reason being, of course, that the practice is becoming widespread.

It is worthwhile noticing that some of the fullest and most competent discussions on the matter are taking place in Israel under the general auspices of the historic Orthodox hospital, Shaare Zedek. The hospital has what one might call a resident Halachist, Eliezer Waldenberg, and he has published a series of volumes. The recent ones are mostly on such questions as artificial insemination, determination of death, etc. In addition to Rabbi Waldenberg, the doctors connected with the Shaare Zedek Hospital conduct a regular seminar on medical Halachic questions. They deal with the latest medical procedures in relation to the Halachah. These seminars are published in pamphlets called "Healing" *(Assia)*. In addition, the editor of the seminar, Dr. Abraham Steinberg, has written two small volumes on these questions *(Lev Abraham)*. Thus all the important other authorities are here cited, as well as providing a unique combination of expert medical competency and Halachic knowledge.

In general, one may say that the situation is as follows: By and large, the authorities insist that the seed, if possible, be that of the husband. To some extent there is some relaxation, but no clear permission for the seed coming from an unrelated donor; although it is accepted, since the seed does not come by actual sexual contact, that the woman receiving the seed from an unrelated donor cannot really be considered an adulteress, though there are some questions as to whether the husband should divorce her or not, and also some questions as to the stage of her menstrual cycle at which these injections should be given.

Let us say, then, that artificial insemination is firmly permitted if the seed comes from the husband. But now the specific question is, suppose that his seed is mixed with other seed. This very question was discussed by Moses Feinstein in his *Igros Moshe (Even Hoezer #71)*. He even used, in Hebrew letters, the word "booster," which means, in this case, strengthening the seed with seed from other donors. Moses Feinstein absolutely forbids this, and so do all the authorities, because it would not be known who could be considered the father. As a matter of fact, Moses Feinstein also objects to this procedure on the ground of deception. The woman believes it is her husband's seed when actually the effective sperm is not from her husband at all.

In the question asked here, the process is much more unacceptable than that of a booster of the husband's seed with the seed of some unknown donor. Here there is added to his seed the seed of his brother and his father, and to the extent that the added seed is the effective seed, which it is meant to be, to that extent it is an incestuous relationship, for the woman is impregnated by the seed of her living husband's brother and/or her husband's father, a totally forbidden incestuous relationship. No wonder this is forbidden by the laws of the state of Michigan; such a mixture should be forbidden by every other state. But it must be stressed again that aside from these especially forbidden mixtures, all mixtures of seed seem to be generally prohibited by all the Halachic authorities who have written on the subject.

THE TEST-TUBE BABY

The news media report the following successful obstetrical experiment in England: A wife, due to malformation of her Fallopian tubes, could not bring the ova down into contact with her husband's sperm. Therefore ova were extracted from her and, in a test-tube, were fertilized by her husband's sperm. The fertilized ovum was then placed into the wife's womb. She carried the fetus to full term and a normal baby was born (by Cesarean operation). Would such a process of fertilization be deemed permissible in Jewish law or tradition? (Asked by a number of inquirers.)

ANSWER:

THE *Medical Tribune* (Vol. 19, #27) reports that tens of thousands of inquiries have come to American physicians since the widespread news of the birth of the "test-tube baby" in England. The *Tribune* adds that it will be quite a long time before such experiments take place in the United States; that is to say, such experiments will, of course, be made with animals but not with humans. The article mentions the fact that the National Institutes of Health have placed a moratorium on federal funding for such experiments on humans until the matter can be reviewed by the National Ethics Advisory Board.

The hesitation by the Ethics Advisory Board clearly

indicates a widespread uneasiness, not only in religious but also in secular circles, about such test-tube experiments with human seed and ova. What can be the basis for such uneasiness? Perhaps an indication of the answer is hinted at in the same article (it is by Wendy Grabel) that when natural fertilization occurs in a woman's body, only one of the innumerable sperms, namely, the most motile sperm, reaches the ovum. Presumably this is the healthiest sperm. But when such fertilization attempts are made in a test-tube, there is no way of knowing which is the healthiest or the most vital of the many sperms. Therefore, it is quite possible that deformed babies, monsters, may result. If, therefore, some bold experimenters dream of using sperm-banks and ovum-banks for the mass production of babies, all sorts of distorted bodies may emerge. We simply do not know, and cannot really know, enough of the results of such an artificial substitute for the natural selection of sperms that can occur in the human body. The National Ethics Advisory Board is therefore quite justified in being extremely cautious, and the Institutes of Health are also justified in declaring a moratorium on such experiments with human sperms and ova.

Curiously enough, some such apprehension (of unnatural results), although in a folkloristic guise, appears in the older Jewish literature. The Talmud (*Nidda* 13b) declares that any man who consciously wastes his seed (either by masturbation or in emissions) is to be considered a murderer. The Biblical text upon which the idea is based is in Genesis 38:8–10, in which Onan, the son of Judah, purposely wasted his seed (from which we get the term "onanism"), and God put him to death for it. The Talmud takes this to mean that Onan was put to death as a murderer. His wasting of the seed was considered equivalent to murder because of the potential lives that that seed might have brought into the world in normal sexual relationships.

The later Kabbalists took this Talmudic warning one step further and said that not only is wasting seed to be considered a sin because of the potential lives that might have been created by it, but actually, say the Kabbalists, certain lives are really created by it. But these are distorted lives, not quite human, or as they say it, *ruchos,* "evil spirits." This Kabbalistic belief in monsters created by the wasted seed led to a specific regulation with regard to funerals in Jerusalem. About one hundred years ago a Kabbalist, Joseph ben Abraham Molcho, forbade his sons to accompany his body to the grave. The reason for his prohibition is given explicitly in the Kabbalistic work *Ha-Kuntres ha-Yechieli,* Vol. II, p. 18b, in which it is explained that in order to keep those monsters (created from wasted seed and who claim to be the man's sons) from going to the funeral, all the sons, even normal ones, are prohibited. This curious custom is still observed in certain Kabbalistic circles in Jerusalem.

This strange Kabbalistic custom, which seems so far-fetched, is not too far-fetched after all, for if scientists should begin to practice wholesale reproduction of humans from sperm and ovum-banks which would be available to them, these "humans" (since we cannot select the most vital sperms) might well turn out to be subhumans, as the Kabbalists declare. The National Ethics Advisory Board, therefore, does well to review this whole possibility with the greatest of care.

However, it must be stated that what was recently

accomplished in England in the Brown case was not at all an attempt at wholesale production of anonymous and unasked-for babies, although potentially the same methods might well be used for such a purpose. The actual purpose of the procedure in England was a specific attempt to be of help to one family in which the mother could not pass the ova because of an obstruction in the Fallopian tubes. Therefore some ova were removed from her and fertilized in a test-tube by her husband's sperm. If, then, this type of procedure is restricted to the one purpose of helping a childless family to have a child, and if the husband's sperm and the wife's ovum (or even an ovum from some donor) are to be used, then this is an entirely different matter and may very well have some limited justification in Jewish law and tradition.

Crucial, then, to this question would now be the actual present status of the family concerned, as to whether or not the husband has already fathered children; for it must be understood that, strange as it may seem, the Jewish religious mandate to have children is a mandate incumbent only upon the man and not upon the woman. Therefore it would not be deemed a sin in Jewish law if a woman remained unmarried, but it is deemed a sin if a man remains unmarried. So, too, a woman may for medical reasons be made sterile, but according to Jewish law, a man who has not yet fulfilled his duty of having a son and a daughter may not be made sterile. If, therefore, a man has already fulfilled his duty of begetting a son and a daughter, and then he marries again and the second wife cannot have children, it would be less likely for the test-tube method to be permitted in this case since the woman is not mandated to have children. But if neither the husband nor the wife have any children, then the test-tube method would perhaps be justified—provided, of course, that the type of procedure in itself can be considered acceptable.

Whether the procedure could be acceptable or not would be difficult to determine definitely, inasmuch as such experiments of mixing husband's sperm with wife's seed outside of the body were unheard of in the past. Perhaps the only way in which we can ascertain the possible attitude of tradition in this matter would be by analogy, or by the implications of certain attitudes which have already been expressed in the past. Let us, therefore, put the question in this way: If the child in the family has not been brought into the world through the normal sexual relationship between the husband and wife, can the child be deemed truly and completely the child of the family involved? The first relevant implication on this matter can be seen in the ancient Biblical institution of Levirate (i.e., brother-in-law) marriage. If brother A dies childless, it is the duty of brother B to marry the widow (Deuteronomy 25:5 ff.). If a child is born of this second marriage, then the child is deemed by Jewish law to be actually the son of the deceased brother A, and he becomes the heir to the estate of brother A, who is considered to be truly his father. Thus we see that a child may be deemed to be the son, in every sense, of a certain man even if not produced by a sexual relationship between his mother and that man.

A second implication of the same kind is to be found in the situation of adopting a child. Is the adopted child considered in Jewish law to be in every sense the child of the adopting parents? The Talmud (b. Sanhedrin 19b) says

that he who raises a child in his house is to be considered
his father. Additionally, the Midrash (*Exodus R*. 46:5)
says that he is the father more truly than the one who
physically begot the child. This may be considered to be
merely a kindly ethical statement. But actually it is a fact in
the strict legal sense. Meir of Rothenburg in his responsa
(#242, ed. Lemberg) says that if a man writing a legal note
refers to an adopted son as "my son," or the son in a note
refers to him as "my father," this is absolutely valid in
every legal sense. This is formally adopted as law (see
Choshen Mishpot 42:15, Isserles). So, again, just as in the
case of a Levirate marriage, we see that a son, even though
not resulting from a normal sexual relationship between
those who are now his parents, is deemed in the fullest
sense a son in Jewish law.

It has been reported in the Jewish press that Rabbi
Goren, the Ashkenazic Chief Rabbi of Israel, has declared
that this test-tube fertilization (if the process is for the
benefit of a childless couple) is acceptable in Jewish law. I
have not seen Rabbi Goren's statement and therefore
cannot know what reasons he may have given for his
affirmative decision. But it well may be that he based his
decision on the two implications mentioned above and
also, of course, on the fact that the duty to have children is
a primary duty in Jewish law, and help should be given, if
necessary, to fulfill that duty.

It might be added that the Talmud (*Chagiga* 15a)
actually refers to a process of an impregnation of a woman
without sexual intercourse. It mentions the possibility that
a man may emit seed in a bathhouse and then a woman,
following there, may be impregnated by that seed, *ibra*

b'ambeti. In fact, there is a tradition that the author Ben Sirach was the child of the Prophet Jeremiah by such a process of impregnation that occurred without any sexual congress. Dr. Harold Cohen, Clinical Professor of Gynecology at the University of Pittsburgh, has informed me that it has happened that a woman was impregnated, even though no sexual intercourse had occurred, when seed was spilled near her body. The Talmudic concept of impregnation in the bathhouse may not be physically real, but it has at least a rather close resemblance to the modern test-tube method of impregnation in a test-tube, outside of the woman's body, or as the physicians would say it, not *in vivo* but *in vitro*.

To sum up: We may say that the concern on the part of governmental authorities and hesitation as to this test-tube process is more than justified. If the process would encourage some experimenters to the wholesale use of sperm and ovum-banks for the artificial production of human babies, one cannot tell what monstrosities might occur. The Kabbalistic notion of monstrous subhumans resulting from wasted seed is at least a picturesque visualization of a real danger.

Since in Jewish law having children is deemed to be a major duty, and if there is a couple who, because of some malformation in the wife's Fallopian tubes, cannot achieve normal fertilization *in vivo,* then, in such a special case, test-tube fertilization and the implanting of the fertilized ovum in the mother's body for pregnancy would be acceptable, since there are other cases in which a child not created by a normal sexual congress is to be accepted in Jewish law as, in the fullest sense, the couple's own child.

Of course, if surgery to straighten the Fallopian tubes or recent attempts at transplanting a Fallopian tube will someday be successful, then these procedures, of course, would be superior to the artificial test-tube method, which then would become unnecessary. So far, unfortunately, since surgery on the Fallopian tubes has not been successful and there is less choice in the matter, the procedure followed in England can be (we might say reluctantly) acceptable.

48

THE TRANSPLANTED OVUM

QUESTION:

The gynecological procedure involved in the question is as follows: A fertilized ovum will be removed from a woman's womb and inserted into the womb of another woman, who will then bear the baby for the full term of months and is expected to give birth to a normal child. The question is, will this baby be considered to be the child of the donor of the fertilized ovum or of the woman who carried it in her womb for full term and gave birth to it? (Asked by Rabbi Harold L. Robinson, Hyannis, Massachusetts.)

ANSWER:

IT IS NOT quite clear whether the procedure described has already been practiced a considerable number of times or whether it is just contemplated and is for the present theoretical. Even if it is only theoretical, it is an interesting and important question because it may become practical (if actually feasible); then, as the practice becomes widespread, it will certainly find strong echoes in the Jewish legal literature. What, then, is (or would be) the Halachic attitude to this procedure of transplanting a fertilized ovum from one woman's womb to another's?

As far as I know, there has not been the slightest mention of such a procedure in the Halachic literature. If the practice becomes known, the earliest mention of it will very likely be in the medical-legal symposia conducted in Israel these days and published under the imprint *Assia*. When the matter *will* be discussed, it is fairly clear that the basic question will be that which is asked here, namely, what is the parentage of the child. It is also clear on what basis the discussion will begin and proceed.

The foundation for this forthcoming Halachic discussion on ovum transplants will be the already well known practice of artificial insemination, which, although also fairly new, has been widespread enough to find considerable discussion in the Halachic literature.

As for this debate on artificial insemination, like all such Halachic debates, it is based upon the Talmud. The Talmud (*Chagiga* 14b–15a) discusses a question based upon the Biblical verse in Leviticus 21:13–14, which states that the High Priest may marry only a virgin. The Talmud then asks this question of Ben Zoma: If a High Priest had married a virgin but then discovered that, although still a virgin, she is pregnant, what is the status of the child, etc.? Ben Zoma is asked how it was possible that this wife of the High Priest could be pregnant and yet remain a virgin. He said that it was possible that she was impregnated in the bath. Rashi explains this answer as follows: In a public bath place, some male bather had emitted semen, and later this young woman, bathing there too, was impregnated by it. (By the way, a gynecologist has implied to me that this Talmudic idea of impregnation without intercourse is quite possible.) This Talmudic idea of a woman thus receiving sperms without sexual intercourse is the basis of all the Halachic debate on artificial insemination. It will also be the basis of the debate on the question you have raised here.

By the way, Dr. Alexander Guttmann of the College faculty and I have both written responsa on artificial insemination. They are found in the *Conference Year Book,* Vol. 62. I will mention now only the two latest responsa on the subject, namely, one by the former Sephardic Chief Rabbi of Israel, Benzion Uziel (in *Mishpotey Uziel, Even Hoezer,* #19), and also one by Moses Feinstein, the most honored American Orthodox respondent, in his second volume on *Even Hoezer* #11. I mention both of these scholars to point out the rather important fact that after perhaps thirty years of Halachic debate, these leading authorities disagree with each other on the basic problem of the child's paternity in artificial insemination. Benzion Uziel is inclined to the opinion that the mother who receives the seed in artificial insemination is the true parent, whereas Moshe Feinstein believes that the donor of the seed in artificial insemination is the true parent.

It might be worth mentioning that Feinstein's decision that it is the donor who is the true parent is not an absolutely firm conviction with him, because, he says, although the donor is to be considered the parent, he is not a parent to the extent that the child born from his donation would free his wife from *chalitza.* That is to say, if a man dies childless, his wife cannot remarry unless her brother-in-law gives her *chalitza,* but if her husband has had a child from any woman (even a woman who was not his wife), the wife is freed from *chalitza.* In other words, Moses Feinstein says that the donor is to be the parent, but not completely so; if he has no other children, his wife must undergo *chalitza* if he dies.

It is, then, upon the basis of the laws developed in the debate over artificial insemination that the question of paternity involved in the ovum transplant will be decided; and since the question of paternity in artificial insemination is still a subject of disagreement between the two prime authorities, we may well say that the question of paternity and inheritance in the case of the ovum transplant is quite open and undecided. It will, of course, have to be cleared up later if the practice becomes widespread, but at present we may say it is an open question.

I am now informed that the actual situation is as follows: The sperm from the husband of the infertile woman is placed in the womb of another woman, the ovum donor, by means of artificial insemination. Thus the ovum of the ovum donor and the sperm of the husband are united and the ovum becomes impregnated. After a brief time, this impregnated ovum is put into the womb of the barren wife and she carries it to full term and a normal baby is then born. As to this situation, it should be mentioned that the mixing of a man's seed with the ovum of a woman not his wife cannot be considered adulterous. If it were adulterous, then the child would be considered a *mamzer*. But it is not adulterous because in this mixture of sperm and ovum there is no *bodily* contact. This decision was already made by many authorities in the case of artificial insemination. So, first of all, it is to be stated that there is no Jewish legal objection to this mixture of sperm and ovum.

As for the parentage of the child, it is almost impossible to come to a definite conclusion on the basis of the Halachah, inasmuch as this situation is totally unprecedented. However, while we cannot be certain, we can speak of the probabilities involved here. In general, the tendency of Jewish law is to emphasize the relation of the child to the *paternal* parent. This is based first upon the Mishnah *Kiddushin* 3:12. The rule there given is as follows: Whenever there is a valid marriage and no sin involved, the child has the status of the male parent. Thus, for example, if a Kohen marries an Israelite woman, such a marriage is both valid and without sin, and therefore the child follows the male and is a Kohen. So, too, if an Israelite marries a Kohen woman, this again is a valid, sinless marriage, and the child again follows the male and is Israelite since his father is Israelite. In other words, the general rule of the law with regard to normal, everyday marriages is that the child has the status of the father. This is discussed in the Talmud, *Kiddushin* 66b–67a. Rashi there explains why, in general, in normal marriages the child follows the status of the father rather than that of the mother. He bases it on Scripture, the first chapter of the Book of Numbers, which says a number of times that the Children of Israel shall be numbered according to their *father's* house.

There is also a second consideration. The fertilized ovum is carried in the womb of the wife for full term. Does the fact that the body matures in the womb of the wife have any bearing on the status of the child? It does, definitely. This can be seen from the special case of a pregnant proselyte. A woman became pregnant while a Christian (presumably pregnant by a Christian man). During her pregnancy, she becomes converted to Judaism. After her conversion, her child is born. What is the status of the child? Is it a Gentile who needs to be converted, since both parents were Gentile? The answer of the overwhelming number of authorities on this matter is that the child is part of the mother's body and the conversion ritual (the *mikvah*) converts not only the mother, but the child that she is carrying (see the authorities cited in the responsum, "The Pregnant Proselyte," in *Modern Reform Responsa,* pp. 143 ff.).

While the situation here is far different from normal marriage, the attitude of the law to normal marriage may serve as an analogy in this special situation. Since the tendency of the law is to emphasize the influence of paternity, and since the wife carries the child and, therefore, according to the law her status impresses itself upon the child, these constitute two reasons why the child here in question should be considered the offspring of the married couple. Of course, as has been said, the situation is unusual, but the likelihood is that as the study of this problem develops, the tendency of the law will likely be to reach the above conclusion.

49

ASSEMBLING A SCHOOL PRAYERBOOK

QUESTION:

Our congregation is planning to assemble a prayerbook for a children's service for the High Holidays. The congregation is not in a financial position to buy a sufficient number of children's prayerbooks which have already been published. It is therefore planning to collect prayers from various sources and mimeograph them as a prayerbook for the use of the children for the holidays. Does this violate Jewish copyright laws (*haskamoth*)? (Asked by Rabbi Sheldon Ezring, Temple Sholom, New Milford, Connecticut.)

ANSWER:

WHAT IS PLANNED here is to collect prayers from various books and thus assemble a prayerbook for children which will be mimeographed and made available for the young people's High Holiday services. The question is asked on the basis of the responsum on copyright in *Contemporary Reform Responsa,* pp. 245 ff., and it amounts to this: Are the authors of the books from which these prayers are to be culled being treated unjustly, since they are deprived of possible profits which they would have if, for example, a hundred books were bought?

The Jewish laws of copyright (*haskama*) did not apply equally to all types of books. While there is no explicit distinction in the legal literature (as far as I know) between one type of book and another as to the right to have a *haskama*, nevertheless in practice there *is* such a distinction. Only such books about which the authors could properly claim that they were the product of their own mind would get a *haskama*. For example, if a man publishes a book of *Chiddushim* on certain Talmudic themes or, let us say, a book of responsa to questions that had been asked him, or a new arrangement of Jewish law in the form of a code, all such books can be properly described as the product of the author's mind for which he has the right to be financially protected (generally for ten years). Even if the book that is published may be considered to be in the *public* domain, such as the Talmud, it may receive a *haskama*. The printing firm in Slavita was given copyright by the rabbis for ten years. And the great dispute that followed the attempt of publishers in Vilna to publish an edition of the Talmud before the ten years were up indicates that there was a special reason for this copyright, although the Talmud is public Jewish property. It was the fact that a vast expense was incurred in the publishing of the Talmud, and it was for this that the publisher deserved to be protected. Unless a publisher got protection after so large an expenditure, then neither he nor other publishers would be likely to publish the Talmud, and the Jewish community would be seriously hampered in its studies. This is the argument made by Moses Sofer in his responsa, *Choshen Mishpot* #41.

However, even for such original books which have had and deserve copyright (*haskama*), it has now become a widespread practice for Orthodox rabbis to have these books (by older authors) reproduced by photo-process.

This reproduction is not necessarily or at all for the use of their own schools or *yeshivos*, but simply for public sale. Such photographing and selling of books of older authors is now a regular, modern business procedure by rabbis unrelated to the older authors. They are simply reproducing these older books for personal profit. Evidently, whatever *haskamoth* the older books had are now deemed to be expired.

So in the case of your congregation's intention, some consideration must be given to the *age* of the books from which the material is to be taken. If the book is, let us say, ten years old or more (which is the usual duration of a *haskama* copyright), we may assume that the author has received his due profit, and we may then freely make a mimeograph of some of the material in it. For this there is ample precedent in the actual practice of many contemporary Orthodox rabbis.

A prayerbook, however, is in a different status from other books, such as *Chiddushim* or responsa. As far as I know, a prayerbook never received a *haskama* preventing other publishers from publishing the prayerbook before the date had passed. There is only one exception of which I know in which a prayerbook had a *haskama*, and that *haskama* was issued by the premier Talmudic authority, Phineas Halevi Horowitz of Frankfurt (1731–1805). This *haskama* was given to protect the *Machzorim* edited by Wolf Heidenheim. But actually it was not given for the prayers themselves—which are, as we might say, in the public domain—but for the remarkably useful commentary made by Heidenheim, explaining the meaning and the sources of the phrases used in the *Piyyutim*. That commentary was the personal creation of Wolf Heidenheim and fully merited copyright protection. But even so, other publishers in Sulzbach and Vienna felt that they were entitled to publish these *Machzorim*, even *with* the commentary of Heidenheim. Whether or not these publishers are to be deemed "pirates" revolves around the question of their right to republish the commentary itself, but if they had published a prayerbook without the commentary, there is no question at all that they had the full right to do so.

As a matter of historical fact, most of the prayerbooks (especially the earlier ones) published in New York for the American Jewish public were simply reprints of prayerbooks printed in Warsaw, Vilna, etc., brought to America by the immigrants. No one, as far as I know, ever raised any objection to this complete republication.

However, if the congregation would be collecting original comments on the *history* of the prayerbook or some special commentary on the prayerbook, there will be a question whether or not permission of the author or publisher should be asked for. But as for the traditional Hebrew prayers themselves, they belong to all of Israel. So does the large literature of Judeo-German and Yiddish prayers in the *Techinos* and similar works. These were written by various authors in comparatively recent centuries. Such books of private devotion were never protected by a "copyright." They have been reprinted at will many times. In fact, almost from the very beginning of this devotional literature *(Techinos)*, there is never a statement of authorship. Clearly, the author of the prayers wrote them with the hope that they would be used by all of Israel.

However, it must be understood that the situation is different with regard to non-Orthodox prayerbooks. These contain new materials, original prayers, creative reworking of older prayers, and often a radical rearrangement of the liturgical structure. Such prayerbooks are to a large extent the product of its author, be it an individual or the committee of a parent organization. As such the prayerbook may well be copyrighted, or even if not formally copyrighted, may justly be considered the property of the author. Therefore, while the intention of the congregation is a worthy one, it being a mitzvah to train children in prayer (*b. Succah* 47a, *Yore Deah* 245:5), nevertheless the congregation must not violate the copyright laws and may not reprint parts of a modern prayerbook without express permission of the author who wrote it or the organization to whom it belongs.

50

MALPRACTICE SUITS AND THE PHYSICIAN

QUESTION:

What is the attitude of the Jewish legal tradition as to medical malpractice suits, which are so prevalent nowadays? (Asked by Dr. Carleton B. Chapman, President, The Commonwealth Fund, New York, New York.)

ANSWER:

BEFORE WE CAN consider the attitude of Jewish law on the specific question of malpractice suits, we must first understand what is the general status of the physician in the tradition. There is an often-cited deprecation of physicians in the last Mishnah of *Kiddushin*, namely, "The best of physicians [should go] to hell." Taken alone, this would seem to express an abysmal contempt for the practice of medicine, an attitude which is unbelievable in the light of the fact that many of the greatest rabbis were also physicians. Actually, the denunciatory passage in the Mishnah discussed is not confined to medicine, but mentions almost every possible occupation and profession of the time, and then dismisses them all with the statement that ends the tractate, namely, that Rabbi Nehorai said: I would abandon *every* livelihood and just teach my child the Torah. Among the livelihoods that are summarily dismissed are such average and normal ones as storekeepers, shepherds, camel-drivers, meat-dealers, and among the whole list, physicians also.

The objection to these livelihoods is explained in the commentary, namely, that each one involves some temptation to sin. The storekeeper is tempted to overcharge, the shepherd to let his sheep graze in someone else's field. As for the physician, the danger in this livelihood is explained by Rashi—that he may forget to be humble in the presence of God and may avoid healing the sick who cannot afford to pay. What the Mishnah, then, really means in this whole listing of livelihoods is: You cannot avoid adopting one of these livelihoods, but beware of the spiritual danger that each one may entail. Therefore it is clear that this denunciation of the physician is not to be taken literally, any more than the denunciation of the storekeeper or the shepherd, etc.

It might be mentioned that this harsh statement also troubled Isaac Lamperonti, himself an honored physician in the city of Ferrara in the eighteenth century. In his encyclopedic work, *Pachad Yitzchok*, under the heading of the statement, "the best of physicians . . . " he says that to the extent that it does apply at all, it might apply only to surgeons who, with the use of instruments, may shed blood more than needed, etc., but it could not apply to physicians who just use medicine. Evidently, Isaac Lamperonti was not a surgeon, but he *was* an honored physician; in fact he was credited with having saved the city of Ferrara in a plague, and the city put an honorary plaque on his house.

The true status of the physician in Jewish legal tradition is clear from the statement given a number of times in the

Talmud, namely, "God gives permission to the physician to heal." The statement is made in commentary of the verse in Exodus 21:19. This "permission" is necessary because God Himself is our true Healer: "I the Lord am your Healer" (Exodus 15:26). Since God is our Healer, then it would be presumptuous for man to usurp God's place. The *Tosfos* (*Baba Kamma* 85a) explains the problem as follows: If someone suffers from a man-made injury, we might understand how a human physician might have the right to cure him, but if he suffers from some God-sent sickness, would it not seem presumptuous for a human being to attempt to undo the act of God? Therefore it is necessary to state what the Talmud does state— that the physician is given divine permission to heal. And, as is further explained, he should not avoid difficult cases and say, "Why should I take the risk of dealing with this invalid? Maybe he will die and I will be accused of carelessness." This he must not say not only because he is a divine emissary, but because healing then becomes a *mitzvah*, a commandment incumbent upon him (cf. *Bes Yosef* to *Tur, Yore Deah* 336).

Just as the physician, being God's emissary, has an inescapable mandate to heal the sick, so does the sick person have a duty to consult a physician and not say, "God will perform a miracle on my behalf" (*b. Shabbat* 32a). He should consult a physician and follow his instructions.

Since the physician is mandated to heal every patient who needs him, it is inevitable that some patients will die under his hands, so it is necessary to consider the direct question that is asked here, namely, to what extent is the physician legally liable for some unfortunate results of his ministrations? There are varying answers to this question, and the legal scholars try to harmonize them into a consistent code of law governing the situation. First of all, it is stated (Tosefta *Gittin* 4:6) that if a patient dies through no malice on the part of the doctor, the doctor is free from guilt. This decision is based upon the general principle that if a man performs a *mitzvah* and in performing it some harm comes inadvertently, he should not be held liable. Thus the Tosefta makes this analogy: If a father strikes a child in disciplining him (which is his duty) and a fatal accident occurs, or if an emissary of the court is sent to flog a culprit and the culprit dies, these men are to be held guiltless. They were performing a duty and they did not intend the unfortunate result. The Tosefta includes the physician in this list because he is performing the *mitzvah* of healing. This freedom from guilt refers to a physician "authorized by the court," which would mean, for our purposes, any authorized physician. "The court would not authorize a physician who is unskilled" (cf. *Tur*, ibid.). This freedom from guilt constitutes an exception in favor of the physician because generally any other man is held liable for his negligence even if no malice was involved; but a physician is not held liable for unintended misfortune. This exception is justified, *mipne tikkun olom*, "for the maintenance, or the establishment, of society." This is explained by David Pardo (cited by Preuss, *Biblisch-Talmudische Medizin*, p. 30) as follows: If physicians would be constantly endangered because of non-malicious error, then no one would risk choosing this form of livelihood and thus the safety of society *(tikkun olom)* would be endangered. Therefore it is a public necessity that the physician be held guiltless in cases of unintended misfortune.

Of course, any physician who with malice aforethought kills or injures a patient is liable to all the punishment and the reparations prescribed by law. Or if he has erred and knows he has erred and realizes that he has been careless, then he must pay the damages as outlined in the law (see the types of reparation, healing, loss of livelihood, pain, etc., all detailed in the tractate *Baba Kamma*).

Because it is difficult to know whether there was serious neglect on the part of the physician, and whether or not he acted to the *best* of his knowledge, the Tosefta therefore adds, he may be free from human punishment, but he will be judged for his neglect by God.

Thus it is evident that this is an area in the law which still needs clarification, and the scholars, as has been said, attempt to achieve it. The fullest discussion of all the elements involved is in the responsa of Simon ben Zemach Duran, Vol. III. Duran himself was a physician in the Balearic Islands in the fourteenth century. Due to the religious persecution in Spain and in the Balearics, he fled to northern Africa, where he became a practicing rabbi because, as he said, the art of medicine was not appreciated by the people. He gives perhaps the fullest statement of all. Nachmanides, a century earlier, also a physician, discusses the matter as has been quoted in his *Toras Ha-Adam* (Venice ed., beginning pp. 12b ff.). The great codes, the *Tur* and the *Shulchan Aruch* (*Yore Deah*

336), give a fairly clear statement of the law. The fullest discussion in modern times is to be found in Preuss, *Biblisch-Talmudische Medizin*.

To sum the matter up, we may say the situation is as follows: The physician is highly honored in the law, and the practice of his profession is a religious duty which he may not evade. For malicious injury he is liable to all the punishments of the law. If there is no malice, but the unfortunate result of the treatment is due to an obvious and realized error that he had made, he is, according to some authorities, liable to damages. For an unintended and unrealized injury, he is held free of punishment even though the average man *is* punished for such unintended negligence. In brief, if there is no manifest malice and no clear and obvious error, the physician is, in Jewish law, free from liability for any unfortunate results of his treatment.

Addendum

The *Sefer Assia,* edited by Dr. Abraham Steinberg in Israel, is a collection of symposia and essays on modern medical practice and Jewish law. On page 283 he has a summary of the various attitudes of the Jewish law on the mistakes that physicians might make and the consequences of them. The summary includes most of the material mentioned above and is summed up by Eliezer Waldenberg, who is, as it were, the resident rabbi of Shaare Zekek Hospital in Israel. He says the following: ''In our time, our conclusion is that no doctor who is not authorized to

practice medicine and is not skilled and has not received a
diploma may practice medicine. Therefore the essence of
the opinions of most of the lines of thought in the Halachah
is expressed by Rabbenu Nissim (above) to free the doctor
under all circumstances'' (see *Tzitz Eliezer,* Vol. V, #23).

51

DEPROGRAMMING YOUNG PEOPLE

QUESTION:

A considerable number of young people, Christian and
Jewish, have deserted the faith of their parents and have
joined various sects, such as Moonies, Hare Krishna, Jesus
Cult, etc. Some parents, deeply grieved at the loss of their
children to these new cults, have turned for help to the newly
developed profession of "deprogramming." These "deprogrammers" sometimes actually kidnap the young people
from their various cult communes and hold them in a sort of
captivity and subject them to "brainwashing" in order to
"cure" them of their delusions. The question asked here is
whether, in the light of Jewish tradition, Jewish parents may
avail themselves of this new method in attempting to win
back the hearts and minds of their young people who have left
them? (Asked by Rabbi M. Robert Syme, Detroit, Michigan.)

ANSWER:

THE QUESTION asked here is based on an entirely modern
situation which has no exact parallel in the past.
Nevertheless, certain elements involved are part of univer-
sal human experience and find reaction in the pages of
Jewish legal and Midrashic literature. That members of the
young generation turn from the faith of their fathers has
certainly occurred many times in the past. An interesting
reaction to this tragic family experience is found in the first

section of the first chapter of *Midrash Rabba* to Exodus.
We are told there that Abraham's older son, Ishmael, was
attracted to idolatrous worship, which, of course, he saw
outside of his father's home; and he followed this practice
and became an idolater. The Midrash, attempting to
explain how the first-born son of the world's greatest
monotheist preferred idolatry, bases its explanation on the
verse in Proverbs 13:24: "He who spares the rod hates his
son." In other words, this happened to Ishmael because
Abraham never disciplined the boy and let him follow his
own predilections. That this is a frequent family experience is indicated by the rest of the Midrash. The Midrash
asks: How was it that Isaac's son, Esau, also picked a way
of life different from his parents? Again the explanation
was given that the boy was never properly taught and
disciplined. The same explanation is given in the same
passage as to why Absalom became a rebel against his
father, David. In other words, the phenomenon of young
people breaking away from the life of the parents is not an
exceptional one, and it is considered in the Jewish tradition
as largely the fault of the parent. The child was not
properly trained and taught.

Of course, this explanation cannot be applied indis-
criminately to all parents in modern occurrences of the
same nature. There are so many new temptations and new
methods of persuasive propaganda that were not available
in the past to bear upon the impressionable minds of the
young. However, parents cannot rid themselves entirely of
some blame for not having provided a sufficiently meaningful religious life. This is certainly true of many modern
Jewish homes.

But whether or not the parents themselves are responsible to some extent, there is no question that they suffer greatly from this new isolation from their children. So they wonder, what can they do to win back the hearts of their Ishmaels and Absaloms. The question, then, arises as to whether the modern professional method of deprogramming is meaningful or acceptable in the spirit of our Jewish religious tradition.

Most of the cults chosen by the youth for their new loyalty seem superstitious or even dishonest to the parents, who find the new cults disgusting or hateful. This disgust or hatred should not be allowed to create a complete estrangement, as can easily occur. Scripture, in Leviticus 19:17, says: "Do not hate thy brother in thy heart, but first reprove thy brother." The duty to find some way to reprove or to teach or to convince is basic in the law. The purpose of such reproving is not to denounce, but to help restore the balance of thought and judgment. The Talmud, in *Pesachim* 113b, discusses the following verse in Exodus 23:5: "If you see the animal of your enemy staggering under his burden, do not turn aside, but help." The Talmud then asks whether this enemy is meant to be a Jewish enemy. But how can it be so, since we are forbidden in Scripture to hate our brother in our heart? The answer the Talmud gives is this: We hate not the person but the sin that we know he has committed, and what the verse directs us to do is, even though we know and hate the sin he has committed, never to refrain from helping as much as we can. This Talmudic discussion is carried on through the tradition and is codified as law in the *Shulchan Aruch, Choshen Mishpot* 272:11. In other words, we have at least this much guidance from tradition, that even if we hate these new cults which we feel have lured our young, we must not permit ourselves to refrain from helping as much as we can.

But is this sort of help, which often involves kidnapping and holding the young person captive, a proper mode of help? In this regard it is well to call attention to the laws concerning the instruction of the young. It is among the primary duties of the parents to train the young to a life of faith and good deeds (*b. Kiddushin* 29b). And by the pedagogic standards of those days, it was considered permissible to use corporal punishment. However, the law is careful to add that under no circumstance may a father use corporal punishment on a *grown* child because the parent will be committing the sin of "putting a stumbling-block in the way of the blind." That particular sin is often discussed in the law, and it means to tempt a person into committing a sin, and what the law here about smiting a grown child means, then, is that the young person will be tempted to retort in anger and perhaps act with violence against his parent, which is, of course, a grave sin (cf. *Tur, Yore Deah* 240, end).

Therefore, hateful as some of these cults are, and serious as is the duty to rebuke, violent methods could well be counter-productive and might alienate the two generations permanently. Jewish tradition, knowing of such alienations in the past, and frequently blaming the laxity of parents for them, imposes the duty to help restore the mental and emotional balance of the estranged youth. But it is evident that the forcible methods of the modern deprogrammers today are contrary to the Jewish ideal of the relation between the generations. May those parents thus afflicted with these estrangements persevere in patience and in hope. There is no easy solution.

52

ALL-ADULT APARTMENTS

QUESTION:

This question is based upon the fact that a young couple living in an "all-adult" apartment house had a baby. The landlord evicted them. The judge upheld the landlord on the ground that ruling against renting rights of parents who have children is not discriminatory under our law, as it would be if the landlord made a ruling against renting rights of people of a certain race or religion. (Rabbi Allen S. Maller, Culver City, California.)

ANSWER:

THERE IS A great deal in Jewish law as to the relationship of landlord and tenant. Most of it, however, deals with the renting of agricultural land. Questions are discussed, for example, as to the different kind of tenant-farming, sharecropping, etc. As for the landlord-tenant relationship in cities, involving the renting of houses or parts of houses, this is discussed to a smaller extent in the law. Most of the law in this matter, beginning with the Talmud, finally is crystallized in the *Shulchan Aruch, Choshen Mishpot* 312 ff.

There the law is absolutely clear that once a lease has been signed, the landlord has no right at all to evict the tenant before the termination of the lease. Even if the landlord's own house collapses and he has no place to live, he cannot argue that it was understood as a precondition:

"If I lost my own home, I could evict you so that I can occupy the house which you have rented from me." He cannot do so.

In fact, Moses Isserles (16th century), in his responsum #19, shows that no such presumed but unspoken conditions can be used by the landlord to oust the tenant before the termination of the lease. In this responsum he deals with the following extreme case: The tenant was to occupy part of the house. The landlord lived in the other part of the house. The lease was signed; but before the tenant moved in, the wife of the tenant contracted yellow fever. The landlord, who lived in another part of the same house, claimed that it was presumed as an unspoken precondition that he surely would not have rented part of his house to a person whose sickness would be a danger to him and his family. Isserles said the landlord cannot use such an argument but must allow the tenant to move in, in spite of the yellow fever which his wife had contracted.

As far as I know, there is only one mention of the question of a family with children. It is as follows: If the tenant wishes to sublease his dwelling or part of it to another family, he may do so provided that the second family is not more numerous than his (*Choshen Mishpot* 316). The commentator Abraham of Bucacz (*Kesef Ha-Kedoshin*) explains this provision on the ground that a larger family would cause more damage than a smaller one. But, he adds, such subleasing to a larger family is forbidden only if the landlord is expected to make the repairs, but if the original renter is expected to make the repairs, then there seems to be no objection to him subletting to a larger family.

As a matter of principle in Jewish law, it would be

unheard of for a landlord to make a condition, as is now
occasionally made, that families with children will not be
given a lease, and that families who have a lease and give
birth to children while they are tenants cannot continue
their lease. Having children is a positive *mandate* of
Scripture. That is why a man is legally in duty bound to
marry. It is a principle in Jewish law that any condition
contrary to the law of the Torah is *ipso facto* void
(*Kiddushin* 19b). Therefore, such a condition would be
ipso facto void in Jewish law. That is why, in all the laws
about rent and tenancy in *Choshen Mishpot,* such a
condition was not mentioned. It would not enter their
minds that a landlord would dare impose such a condition.

53

THE "UNWANTED" CHILD

QUESTION:

From the point of view of Jewish legal tradition, under what circumstances may an "unwanted" child be given up for adoption? (Asked by Paul A. Flexner, Youngstown, Ohio.)

ANSWER:

PERHAPS A BETTER term than "unwanted" should be used to describe the child, because it well may be that the mother would very much want to keep the child but for many reasons is unable to do so. Then the question might be rephrased as follows: Under what circumstances, according to Jewish law, may a mother give up a child for adoption?

There is a great deal of evidence in literature that children were given up by their parents. The Mishnah and the Talmud have a long sequence of legal development about children who have been abandoned by their parents. There are two classes of such children (both described in the Mishnah *Kiddushin* 4:2): One, *shetuki,* from the root meaning "silence"; this refers to children who are old enough to know their mother but do not know (i.e., there is silence about) their father. The other, *asufi,* are infants of whose parentage nothing is known.

In the discussion of these abandoned infants, the law

gives a sort of an acceptance of the necessity which led the parent or parents to abandon the infant. The law reads that if it is in time of famine, then we assume that the parents have abandoned the child because they are no longer able to take care of him and they hope that someone will pick up their child and feed it (*Kiddushin* 73b, *Even Hoezer* 4:31). In other words, applying this to modern times, one reason for giving up a child would be if the parent or parents are unable to take care of the child and to raise it.

There is, of course, another motivation on the part of a modern parent to give up a child besides the motivation—which, alas, is not too infrequent—of the lack of means to maintain it. There is the sense of shame on the part of a young unmarried woman at having borne a child out of wedlock. The element of shame is an important consideration in Jewish law. If one person injures another, besides the pain and the healing for which the assailant must pay, he must also pay for the shame, if such is involved (*Choshen Mishpot* 420:3). In fact, shame is counted as one of the leading forms of injury. Among the types of shame mentioned in the law (*Ketubos* 3:4) is the shame caused either by rape or seduction. While the law does not discuss the possibility of a young woman in these circumstances giving up the child for that reason, it is obvious that among the *asufi* and *shetuki,* the abandoned children, many were abandoned, not only because of hunger, but because of shame. This, too, might therefore be considered a justification for giving up a child for adoption, even though it is not expressly mentioned, as hunger is mentioned, as a reason for giving up of the child.

There is one possible modern reason today which would

not be supported by the tradition, and that is the special motivation to get rid of a child because it is illegitimate. In the first place, at least three-quarters of the infants considered by modern English and American law as illegitimate, would not be illegitimate according to Jewish law. In Jewish law, only the offspring of a union which cannot be made legal is illegitimate. For example, the offspring of an incestuous relationship, or the offspring of a relationship between a man and another man's wife, these relationships cannot be legalized by a marriage at the time and such offspring only are illegitimate. But the offspring of a union with an unmarried girl (not a close relative) is, according to Jewish law, legitimate. Furthermore, while in all cultures illegitimate children are under some stigma and in Jewish law an illegitimate may not marry into a normal family, this latter is actually the only stigma. An illegitimate (even in the restricted Jewish sense) may be a judge, may be a witness, is bound to all the commandments as other people are.

Therefore it is not likely that Jewish law would provide any justification for giving up an infant merely because it is illegitimate. However, it must be granted that in modern times and in modern society, the shame involved in having an illegitimate child is not in accordance with the liberal Jewish definition, but in accordance with the understanding of the environment in which the mother lives. The mother may well want to give up the child for this reason, but Jewish law has no specific support for it.

There is one additional justification in modern life for giving up a child for adoption. Roman law provided a regular legal system of adoption from one family to another. In Jewish law there was no such regular legal system. Nevertheless, one who raises another's child—in other words, adopts him or her—is highly praised for it (*Sanhedrin* 19b). Examples are given in the Talmud of such private adoptions, even though there was no regular legal system for it. But today, there is a regular social organization for adoption, and whereas in the old days, in time of famine, a child might be left on the street in the hope that a worthy person would pick it up, nowadays prospective adoptive parents are examined and only if found worthy are given the child. Therefore there would be an additional justification today for giving a child up for adoption.

To sum up: The justifications for giving away a child are in Jewish law two clear ones: one, "hunger," the inability to nourish the child; two, shame at having had the child. The permission is strengthened by the modern method of the careful selection of adopting parents.

INQUIRIES

1

INQUIRY

HALACHAH AND SPACE TRAVEL

QUESTION:

The religious school of the temple is engaged in gathering material for a discussion of the relationship of Jewish religious tradition and mankind's new experience with space. What material is there in the Halachah that can be useful for such a study? (Asked by Rabbi Albert M. Lewis, Grand Rapids, Michigan.)

ANSWER:

THE QUESTION is, of course, primarily an exploration of Jewish thought rather than a search for practical guidance, since there cannot be many Jewish astronauts to whom the problems might apply. It might be interesting at the outset to note the potentially different attitudes of Judaism and Christianity on the problem of the applicability of the respective religions to outer space. Theologically the problem might be more difficult for Christianity than for Judaism. The essence of Christian theology is concentrated on this earth. It is on this earth alone that Christianity believes that God Himself was incarnated. The drama of salvation is, therefore, concentrated in what we now know is a tiny planet in one of the smaller of the millions of solar systems. How can it be explained theologically that the central drama of Christianity is concentrated in this speck of earth lost in the entire vast universe?

In regard to this theological question, Judaism has fewer difficulties to meet. The earth and humanity, while important in Jewish thought, are not at all central. The Midrash which expresses our attitudes makes of the whole creation of man and the whole giving of the Torah something much greater than this earth and the human race. That is why we are told that the angels argued with God against the very creation of the earth, and argued more strongly against the giving of the Torah to human beings (see the material gathered in the first volume of Ginzberg's *Legends*). In other words, God's world and God's dominion and God's plans include much more than this little earth and its people.

It is worth noting which Biblical phrases are brought into the regular worship and how they insist upon the larger universe. In the daily service, we speak of God as Master of *all worlds* (a phrase used by Rabbi Yochanan in *Yoma* 87b). In the daily service we have the psalm (147:4): "He numbereth the stars and calls them each by name." In the Sabbath Torah service, we use the sentence (from I Chronicles 21:11): "Everything in heaven and earth is Thy kingdom." In other words, the mood of Judaism, different from that of Christianity, does not concentrate God's plan on this little planet, but constantly emphasizes the vast universe as God's dominion. Thus it is clear that on the basis of general theology it is less difficult for Judaism to face the modern astronomical view of a vast expanding universe.

However, while it will be theologically easier for Judaism than for Christianity to confront the new questions of vast space, *practically,* however, with regard to the regulation of life, Judaism would have a much more difficult task of adjustment than Christianity. That is because, as far as ceremonies and observances are concerned, Judaism is full of regulations based upon time and space which would seem impossible to adjust to the new astronautic techniques. For example, in the laws of travel on the Sabbath, *space* is divided in Jewish law as to how *far* a man may travel. Also, as to carrying on the Sabbath there are definite limits. Then there are questions as to food and work. Let us take some of these questions up in order.

The question of carrying on the Sabbath is no question at all for the astronaut because everything in the capsule is weightless. The question of adjusting machinery on the Sabbath is not difficult either because it is a matter of saving life, for which all is permitted. The question of food, on the assumption that the concentrated food is not kosher, again this is permitted because of the danger to life. The astronaut is under compulsion to eat that food and, as a matter of fact, when one eats forbidden food under necessity in place of danger, he is even in duty bound to pronounce the blessing over the food (*Orach Chayim* 196:2).

The only question that is more difficult with regard to space travel is the question of the Sabbath journey. According to the rule, a man may walk throughout his city on the Sabbath and two thousand cubits beyond its limits.

From then on, he may only move four cubits. However, the astronaut covers vast distances. He goes around the earth in eighty minutes. How is that permissible on the Sabbath? The answer is clear enough: None of the Sabbath limits of travel apply beyond the height of ten cubits above the earth. Therefore it is permitted to travel on the Sabbath on the ocean because the ship is more than ten cubits above the earth. The astronaut may cover any distance on the Sabbath because of the height above the earth.

One last question remains, however: The astronaut goes around the earth in eighty minutes. He sees the dawn every forty minutes and sunset every forty minutes. How, then, can he manage morning and evening prayers? What about the morning *tallis* and *tefillin* for an Orthodox astronaut? He certainly cannot be expected to put them on every forty minutes throughout his journey. The answer to this problem must be the same as that which was given to the soldiers in Iceland during the war: Since it was dark there for six months and then light for six months, how could they have evening services at sunset? The answer to that problem was that they must follow the hours of Boston, Massachusetts, and the soldiers in Alaska must follow the hours of Portland, Oregon. After all, the watches in the space capsule will keep earth time.

This, for the present, seems to be all that comes to mind with regard to space travel.

2

INQUIRY

SALT FOR THE BREAD BLESSING

QUESTION:

Is it required to have salt on the table when the blessing over bread is made, and is it required, also, that the bread be dipped into the salt? (Asked by L.S.F.)

ANSWER:

FROM THE VERY beginning, salt was a very important part of the ritual. The sacrifices in the Temple (and before that in the Tabernacle in the Wilderness) could not be offered without salt. Leviticus 2:13 reads, "And every meal-offering of thine shalt thou season with salt; neither shalt thou suffer the salt of the covenant of thy God to be lacking from thy meal-offering; with all thy offerings shalt thou offer salt." Numbers 18:19, speaking of offerings, reads in a general way, "It is an everlasting covenant of salt before the Lord unto thee and to thy seed with thee." Thus salt was considered to be a symbol of God's covenant with Israel in general.

From the idea that the salt with the sacrifices was a symbol of the covenant with God, there was a logical transition to believe that also at the blessing over bread, as

with sacrifices on the altar, salt should be present as a
symbol of covenant with God. Thus the Talmud, speaking
of the one who breaks bread (i.e., the one who makes the
blessing of the bread for the company, breaking off a piece
of the loaf for the blessing) says as follows, "The one who
breaks bread is not permitted to break the bread until they
bring him salt or condiment [*lifton*]" (*Berachos* 48a).

However, two facts are to be noticed about this statement. First, the condiment need not necessarily be salt—it
could be any other condiment that the bread could be
dipped in; and secondly, the rabbi, Rava Bar Samuel, who
is the author of the statement, ate a meal at the house of the
Exilarch and made the blessing over the bread without any
salt. When asked whether he had changed his mind as to
his former requirement that there should always be salt at
the blessing over the bread, he said that it was not
necessary here to delay the blessing (i.e., to wait for salt).
This Rashi explains by saying that it was good bread and
did not require any condiment. In fact, the *Tosfos* to the
passage says, "We are not accustomed to bring on our
table either salt or other condiment because our bread is of
high quality."

The same ambiguity as to requiring salt is reflected in
the law as given in the *Shulchan Aruch*. In *Orach Chayim*
167:5, Joseph Caro first states the law as given in the
Talmud, namely, that salt or other condiment must be
brought so that the one who gives the blessing can dip the
bread into it. But then Joseph Caro continues by saying
that if it is pure bread, already seasoned "as our bread is,"
it is not necessary to wait for salt to be brought. However,
Isserles says as follows, "At all events, it is a *mitzvah* to

have salt on the table before the blessing is made, because our table is like the altar and our food is like a sacrifice, and it is said 'and all thy sacrifices thou shalt bring salt.' "

To sum up, it is not an absolute requirement to dip the bread in salt, especially if the bread does not require the condiment. However, because of the association with the sacrifices on the altar, which always did require salt, Isserles states it is proper to have the salt. It is clear that those who omit using the salt, if their bread is of good quality and well seasoned, do not actually violate any law.

3

INQUIRY

HYPNOTISM

QUESTION:

Is hypnotism as a therapeutic method permitted in Jewish law? (Asked by Sonia Syme, Detroit, Michigan.)

ANSWER:

THE PROCESS of putting a person to sleep was known in ancient India and in ancient Persia, but the idea of using this medically was created by Mesmer (hence "mesmerism") just two centuries ago in Vienna. I mention this dating so you can understand that Jewish law could know nothing about it.

But, of course, one might say that there is a good example of it in the Bible. When God wanted to remove a rib from Adam to create Eve, we are told He put him into a deep sleep; and the Ramban (Nachmanides), who was also a physician, said that God put him into a deep sleep in order that he should not feel the pain of the operation. In other words, we might call this hypnotism as a means of anesthesia.

Again, in Scripture, God was involved with a human being falling into a deep sleep. That was in the case of

Abraham, when God made a special covenant with him
(Genesis 15:12 ff.). We are told there that the deep sleep
came upon Abraham, accompanied by a feeling of great
terror, and in this sleep God revealed to him the exile of his
children as slaves in Egypt, and the Midrash to the passage
says that in that sleep there was revealed to him all the
exiles (four of them) that would take place in the future. So
here God used deep sleep, not as an anesthetic as with
Adam, but as a means of transmission of ideas.

Whether these two cases could serve as an indication of
the permissibility of hypnotism, one cannot say. However,
this must be stated as a general principle: If it is a patient
who is dangerously sick, the Sabbath, which is the strictest
of all laws, must (not may) be violated in his behalf, and all
other prohibitions in the law, such as kosher food, etc.,
may be violated for him.

So without stressing the two narratives mentioned
above, we might say that certainly hypnotism or any other
remedy is permissible in Jewish law for a patient who is in
a dangerous condition.

4

INQUIRY

REFORM AND SPIRITUALISM

QUESTION:

> There has been a considerable increase of interest in spir-
> itualism (seances, mediums, etc.) here in South Africa.
> What is the attitude of Reform Judaism to these practices?
> Is it the same as that of Orthodox Halachah? (Asked by
> Rabbi Paul Liner, Pretoria, South Africa.)

ANSWER:

FIRST OF ALL, it is necessary to understand fully the
attitude both of the Halachah and also of Jewish popular
tradition as to the question of communication with the
dead. The Bible is absolutely clear that evoking the dead in
order to communicate with them is considered a sinful
practice equivalent to idolatry. See Leviticus 19:31, 20:6
and 27, and especially Deuteronomy 18:10 and 11. As for
the incident in the Book of Samuel where the Witch of
Endor summons up the spirit of the Prophet Samuel, that
act was performed by a witch and certainly was not cited
with approval.

The later law maintains this prohibition. The Mishnah in
Sanhedrin 7:7 and the Talmud in *Sanhedrin* 65a state that
the medium who summons the dead has committed a

capital offense and should be punished by stoning. The inquirer of the medium should receive a warning not to repeat this sin. Maimonides (*Hil. Avoda Zara* 11:13) says that he who summons the dead to communicate should be punished. So the law stands in the *Shulchan Aruch, Yore Deah* 179:1, giving the general prohibition against astrology, and in 179:13 the law prohibits any attempt to summon the dead.

However, although the law is clear that to attempt any such communication with the dead is strictly forbidden, nevertheless the popular feeling persisted that it was possible to converse with the dead (even though summoning them to return was forbidden). Thus the *Shulchan Aruch,* after definitely forbidding the practice of summoning the dead, states that it is permitted to ask a dying person to return to communicate with the living. This permission is given by the *Hagahos Maimoniyos* to the passage quoted above from the Code of Maimonides. The basis for this permission is found in two incidents in the Talmud (*Moed Katan* 28a). Rabbi Searin was at the bedside of his dying brother Rava, and he made such a request of him, namely, that he return to him in a dream. The same request had previously been made by Rava when he was at the bedside of the dying Rabbi Nachman. But, of course, asking a dying person to appear to us in a dream is far different from having a medium (presumably) summon the dead, as the Witch of Endor did with the Prophet Samuel.

In Jewish folk feeling, there is an even greater communication with the dead than their appearing in our dreams. The widely established Jewish custom of going to the cemetery and praying at the graveside might appear to be a sort of a summoning of the dead to communicate with us. Therefore Joel Sirkes (the *Bach*), at the end of *Tur, Yore Deah* 217, finds it necessary to defend the practice of praying at the graveside. He says it has by now become an established custom and need not be considered as violative of the command "not to inquire of the dead." As a matter of fact, the custom of praying at the graveside for help from the dead has a Talmudic precedent. The Talmud, commenting on the verse in Numbers 13:22, that the twelve spies came to Hebron, says that Caleb prayed there on the graves of the patriarchs to be saved from the evil machinations of the other spies (excepting, of course, Joshua) (Sota 34b).

As to the prayers recited when visiting the grave, there has developed over the years a fairly large prayer-literature. The best known collection of these prayers is the book *Ma'aney Loshon*. A study of the prayers in this book will show that even in these prayers, which appeal to the simple, unsophisticated people, there is a definite restraint in the expression of relationship to the dead. In most of the prayers, the dead are not directly spoken to. The prayers are addressed to God, asking Him that He should listen to the departed when they plead in behalf of the living. The idea that the dead plead with God in behalf of the living has given rise to the phrase often used by pious women, referring to a dead parent, "May he be a good advocate for us." The dead would be praying for the welfare of the living (a recurrent theme in these prayers). This is presumed to take place in heaven, a far different idea from mediums summoning the dead to come to us. Whenever the dead *are* directly addressed, as they are occasionally in these prayers, it is to express the wish that they may rest in peace in their graves. But nearly all the direct petitions are made to God Himself.

To sum up the traditional attitude, the law forbids any attempt to summon the dead. But the feeling of the people—one might say, the folklore—is that the dead may be communicated with at their graveside and prayers addressed to God that the dead may intercede with Him in behalf of the living. That is as far as even Jewish folklore goes as to contact with the dead.

The attitude of Orthodox tradition makes the Reform attitude clear. In general, Reform was the product of the Enlightenment and maintained only such customs as could stand in the light of reason. Therefore in Reform prayerbooks the prayers to the dead have undergone a subtle but a definite change. In Reform memorial services, the departed are honored in memory and the hope is expressed that their good example may ennoble our lives, and gratitude also is voiced for their loving-kindness to us in their lifetime.

Thus the small amount of pleading for the help of the departed which remains in Orthodox popular faith, even this has been dropped out in all Reform prayerbooks; so certainly the firm prohibitions of the Halachah against direct mediumistic evocation of the spirits of the dead would be equally honored in Reform.

5

INQUIRY

REFORM AND MAMZERUS

QUESTION:

The law in South Africa allows a man to marry his brother's divorced wife. Such a marriage was contracted and a child was born of it. But according to the Halachah, a man may not marry his brother's wife (Leviticus 18:16), hence the child is a *mamzer*. Does Reform Judaism adhere to all the strict Orthodox laws against the rights of *mamzerim*? (Asked by Rabbi Isaac Richards, Temple David, Durban, South Africa.)

ANSWER:

THERE IS NO doubt that according to the Halachah a man may not marry his brother's wife. This is clearly stated in the list of prohibited marriages which are considered incestuous in Leviticus 18:16. Yet even this marriage, which is counted as incestuous, can sometimes not only be permitted, but is even considered to be a religious duty. That would be in the case where the brother dies childless. So it is clear that this prohibited marriage is somewhat different in its essence than the other prohibited marriages listed in Leviticus. However, since the brother did not die childless (at least I assume so), then the marriage is indeed a prohibited one and the child is a *mamzer*. The essential question asked is, what is the attitude of Reform Judaism to such a child?

First, it is necessary to clear up certain misapprehensions about the status of the *mamzer* in traditional Jewish law and life. A certain Gentile novelist, who wrote a novel about ancient Israel, described the *mamzer* as being an outcast, a pariah, scorned and rejected by all. This is far from the case.

The actual status of the *mamzer* in Jewish law is as follows: Scripture says (Deuteronomy 23:3): "He shall not enter the congregation of the Lord." The word " congregation" here means, of course, "community," and it means specifically that he may not marry into a legitimate Jewish family. But even this prohibition is limited. He *may* marry a convert because converts (at least in the first generation) are considered to be a separate *kahal* or "congregation," and into *this* congregation of Jews, he may marry.

This prohibition of marriage is the *only* disability which a *mamzer* endures. For example, he is entitled to be a witness in the Jewish courts *(kosher l'edus) (Choshen Mishpot* 34:21). He may be circumcised, even on the Sabbath *(Yore Deah* 265:4), where the explanatory statement is made, "A *mamzer* is like any other Israelite". He may be called up to read the Torah before the congregation *(Orach Chayim* 282:3, note of Isserles). If his brother dies childless, he is in duty bound, like any "legitimate" brother, to marry the widow or give her *chalitza* (Mishnah *Yevamos* 2:5, explained in the Talmud, *Yevamos* 22a). When the father dies, he is an equal heir with the other "legitimate" brothers (Mishnah *Yevamos* 2:5, Talmud *Yevamos,* ibid., which makes the statement that he is a brother in every respect—*ochiv l'chol dovor*—and this is codified in the law as in *Choshen Mishpot* 276:6). And, of course, aside from all these rights, the statement is well known (Mishnah *Horayos* 3:8): "A learned *mamzer* is deemed superior to an ignorant High Priest."

So from the above it is clear that even in the strictest Orthodox law, except for the right to marry into a regular family, a *mamzer* has all human and Jewish rights. Thus, if the question were asked of the strictest Orthodox authority, the above would be the answer. Indeed, under certain special circumstances, it is conceivable that Orthodox authorities would also remove any stigma from this girl. The best-known Orthodox authority in the United States, Moses Feinstein, was faced with the fact that a young woman had been divorced in the courts and could not secure a *get* from her husband (who was unavailable). Feinstein found out that the girl had been married by a Reform rabbi, and so he decided as follows: The marriage ceremony conducted by a Reform rabbi lacked the presence of kosher witnesses (Sabbath observers, etc.), therefore the marriage was null and void, and the young woman did not need a *get* at all *(Igros Moshe, Even Hoezer,* new series). So if the brother who was the first husband had been married by a Reform rabbi, Moses Feinstein might, in an emergency at least, declare that marriage void, and therefore the wife was not really a wife and could very well marry the brother, and the little girl would not be a *mamzeres* at all. But this decision of Moses Feinstein is a bold and a dangerous one.

Now the question asked is: What would be or should be the attitude of Reform Judaism as to the status of this child born of the above-mentioned marriage? We must consider the fact that Reform, from the very beginning, took a bold, revolutionary attitude in the field of marriage when it accepted the full validity of civil divorce. Orthodoxy, which does not consider any Jewish marriage dissolved without a valid Jewish *get,* would consider any marriage undertaken by a woman after a civil divorce an immoral marriage and utterly invalid. Therefore, the children of the second marriage are *mamzerim* in Jewish law. At this stage in Jewish social history, it is not only among Reform families, but there are innumerable numbers of other families in which there has been a remarriage without a Jewish *get.* Who, now, would dare to declare perhaps half of western Jewry to be technically illegitimate? Even Orthodox rabbis, unless the matter is plainly and inescapably put before them, would not hesitate to marry any average Jewish couple.

In actual historical effect, Reform has led the way to removing the stigma of *mamzerus* from countless Jewish individuals. You might say, therefore, that without openly declaring the principle that the concept of *mamzerus* is no longer operable today, Reform has simply taken no notice of it. Of course, perhaps in Reform we should be hesitant in ignoring such *mamzerus* as is due to actual incest. But perhaps, even so, we should consider the child innocent. But certainly in such cases where no actual incest (i.e., not of consanguinity but only of affinity) is involved, Reform follows the principle in the Talmud *Kiddushin* 76b that ''all families are presumed to be kosher.'' Of course, this means that they are presumed to be kosher unless the question is formally raised about them, which, as far as we are concerned, we will not do.

To sum up: The child in question is indeed in Halachah a *mamzeres*, but even so, as we have seen, she has in the Halachah every right of a Jewish child except that of marrying into a regular family. Reform, which has removed the stigma of remarriage without a *get*, certainly would not allow this stigma to be put upon the child.

Addendum

Moses Feinstein is not the only American Orthodox authority who denies the validity of Reform marriage. Menashe Klein, dean of a yeshiva in Brooklyn, in Vol. VII of his *Mishne Halachos (Even Hoezer* #214) likewise declares Reform marriages invalid. Whereas Feinstein was concerned with a woman who could not obtain a *get*, Klein is concerned with the subject of our discussion, namely, *mamzerus*.

He was asked by a scholar in Jerusalem whether it is permissible to officiate at marriages in which one party or both are of Reform Jewish families. He answers that the problem involved is due to the fact that Reform Jews accept the validity of civil divorce, while according to Jewish law a civil divorce is not a divorce at all. Therefore, if the woman was civilly "divorced" and remarries, the marriage is not lawful according to Jewish law, and the children born of this second "marriage" are *mamzerim*, who therefore may not marry into a normal Jewish family.

However, he does not believe that this taint of *mamzerus* is a serious obstacle to marrying people of Reform families. First of all (he says), the majority of families do not divorce, and as to the minority which *has* divorced in the courts, an official public record is available of those proceedings, and such families can be, therefore, easily identified.

Then he goes further and uses a rabbinical phrase which may be freely translated as follows: "Their disadvantage redounds to their advantage." What he means is this: Since Reform marriages lack kosher witnesses, they are invalid, which is the same statement as made by Moses Feinstein (a "kosher" witness is one who obeys the Torah laws and the Rabbinic laws; cf. *Choshen Mishpot* 34:2–3 and Isserles). Therefore, he says, the first marriage was not valid, and the woman who was divorced in the civil court never needed a divorce at all, and therefore her so-called second marriage is really her first marriage and the children are not illegitimate.

In other words, the implications of the denial of validity to Reform marriages by both Feinstein and Klein really amount to this: that there is perhaps less *mamzerus* in the Reform Jewish community than in some other sections of the Jewish people. In fact, Klein in responsum #211 says specifically, for the aforementioned reasons, that Reform families are to be considered legitimate and marriageable with pious Jewish families (p. 139, top of col. 2).

6

INQUIRY

FUNERAL FOLKLORE: KEYS IN THE COFFIN

QUESTION:

A bereaved family insisted that their deceased father's keys be put into his hand, to be buried with him. Is there any justification for this custom? (Asked by Louis J. Freehof, Sinai Memorial Chapel, San Francisco, California.)

ANSWER:

THERE IS AN understandable tendency for strange customs to grow up around the process of burial. The surviving relatives are so anxious to do everything they can do for their deceased dear one that almost any practice that they hear about they would tend to observe. It is for this psychological reason that the authorities are especially alert to avoid any unjustified practice or observance.

However, this particular practice of putting a key in the hand of the deceased does happen to have some vague rootage in Jewish law and tradition. In the post-Talmudic booklet *Evel Rabassi (Semachos* 8:7), there is the following statement: "We may loosen the hair of brides [who have died], uncover the faces of bridegrooms [usually the faces of the dead are covered], and hang the deceased's key and ledger book on the coffin because of grief." Then it adds that when Samuel Ha-Katan died, they hung his key and his ledger on his coffin because he had no child (hence there was special grief by his colleagues at his death). This statement is repeated by Asher ben Yechiel in his code *(Moed Katan* 3:81). His son, Jacob ben Asher, repeats this statement in his code, the *Tur (Yore Deah* 350), and Joseph Caro carries it over in the *Shulchan Aruch (Yore Deah* 350).

However, it is to be observed that this chance custom of the deceased's keys and ledger being buried with him is deprecated by Joel Sirkes (the *Bach)* in his commentary to the *Tur.* He says this is a mistaken custom—we do not observe it, and we should prevent people who want to observe it. This warning of the *Bach* against the custom is repeated by the *Be'er Hetev* to the *Shulchan Aruch.*

The custom of putting the keys with the dead, referred to in this question, is objectionable from another point of view. The custom of burying the key and the ledger, mentioned above and strongly objected to by the *Bach,* really was that these things were put in or hung outside of the coffin and not put into the hand of the deceased. Closing the hand of the deceased around any object or even just clenching the hand without an object in it is objectionable to law and custom.

The following is the statement by the *Kitzur Shulchan Aruch* (197:5): "It is necessary to be watchful that the dead should not close his hands. As for the custom in some cases to close the fingers, this custom must be abolished. Also, that some put into his hand rods they call *geplach,* this is a foolish custom."

(By the way, the custom of twigs of *geplach* put into the

hands of the deceased is evidently symbolic of having a cane or walking stick at the time of the Resurrection.)

To sum up: The custom of putting keys into the hands of the deceased is objectionable, therefore, on two grounds: first, that the *Bach* prohibits the custom as being against our prevailing usage, and second, because it involves clenching the hands of the dead, which is also objectionable.

7

INQUIRY

CHAROSES

QUESTION:

A friend found the *charoses* difficult to digest because of the presence in it of rough ingredients, perhaps like shells of nuts. Is it necessary to have such material to make up the bulk to fulfill the requirements of the *mitzvah?* (Asked by Rabbi Mark Staitman.)

ANSWER:

THE BASIC question involved is whether the *charoses* is a *mitzvah* that requires a blessing. If it is, then there must be a certain definite bulk to it, at least to the amount of an olive, for a blessing to be recited. The question as to whether it is a *mitzvah,* and therefore requires a blessing and the bulk of at least an olive, is discussed at the very earliest stage of the Halachah. In the Mishnah in *Pesachim* 10:2, one rabbi says it is not a *mitzvah* and another rabbi says it is. The discussion is continued through the Talmud, and finally Maimonides concludes (*Hil. Chometz* 7:11) that it is a *mitzvah,* not in the Torah sense but in the Rabbinic sense. This leaves open the question whether it needs a blessing, because some Rabbinic *mitzvahs* do require a blessing and some do not. The final conclusion is that it does not require a blessing, and *Maharil* is cited to this effect (see the opinions marshaled in *Pachad Yitzchok*, s.v., *charoses*). The reason given is that the herb does not require a blessing and the *charoses* is merely secondary to it or auxiliary to it. Therefore, since it requires no blessing, it requires no special amount, and the rough material can be left out without question.

By the way, the recipe for *charoses* is discussed by Isserles in *Orach Chayim* 473:5. You will find it interesting that Bertinoro, who was Italian, speaks of figs as its basic material, and Isserles speaks of apples. In the *Shulchan Aruch,* Caro is careful that the herbs be the proper amount, but Isserles does not mention any amount.

8

INQUIRY

DISTRIBUTION OF LAWS IN JEWISH LEGAL LITERATURE

QUESTION:

With regard to the distribution of laws in Jewish legal literature, as to how many there are in the various codes in their chronological succession; that is to say, how many are there in the *Mishna Torah,* how many in the *Shulchan Aruch,* etc.? (Rabbi Allen S. Maller, Culver City, California.)

ANSWER:

IF YOU MEAN how many were added in the various codes, this question is impossible to answer, because it was a fixed doctrine, mentioned clearly in the Talmud, that all the 613 commandments are in the Torah itself. In *Maccos* 23b the doctrine is based on the verse in Deuteronomy 33:4, *"Torah tsiva lonu Moshe,"* which means that the word *Torah* itself numerically adds up to the number 613. In other words, all of the commandments are already given in the Torah itself. And notice, too, that Aaron of Barcelona (13th century) wrote a book, *Sefer Ha-Chinuch,* showing how all the commandments are connected and derived from the Torah. And this book was expanded in the last generation to a still larger book, *Minchas Chinuch,* by Joseph Babad.

Of course, it sometimes required careful homiletics in the Halachic Midrashim and in the Talmud to prove the Biblical derivation of certain commandments, but they proved it to their satisfaction.

Perhaps the question should be asked as follows, and perhaps this was the intention of your question, namely, not which commandments were *added* in the later codes, but which were *omitted* from them. This can be more directly answered. Maimonides included all of them, even the detailed laws of the animal sacrifices in the Temple. Jacob ben Asher in the *Tur* omitted the Temple and the Palestinian agricultural laws. In other words, he left out all laws which could not be observed in the Diaspora. In this he was followed, of course, by Joseph Caro in the *Shulchan Aruch.*

As a practical fact of modern life, it must be added that nearly all the business laws are fading away. You rarely find a question on *Choshen Mishpot* in present-day responsa volumes. In fact, if you will look on the front page of the Vilna editions of the *Shulchan Aruch,* you will find a statement that most of the *Choshen Mishpot* laws are no longer in practice. I remember that Schechter, in his *Studies in Judaism,* has an essay on the 613 commandments in which he records many of them as no longer in actual observance. My answer to you, therefore, is as follows: By theory, all 613 were found in the Torah, but then they gradually diminished as indicated above.

Combined Index for Reform Responsa (I), Recent Reform Responsa (II), Current Reform Responsa (III), Modern Reform Responsa (IV), Contemporary Reform Responsa (V), Reform Responsa for our Time (VI), New Reform Responsa (VII)

Abortion:
    and German measles, II, 188
    and live fetus study, VI, 256
    CCAR, II, 188
Adoption:
    baptism of adopted child before, II, 97
    by Kohanim, V, 145
    children of mixed races, III, 196
    two problems, V, 86
Aguna: I, 86
All-adult apartments, VII, 236
Answers:
    to CCAR Journal, III, 214
    to Israel on conversion, V, 269
    to Social Security Office, III, 209
Apostate:
    attitude to, IV, 169
    burial of, II, 127
    daughter of, I, 192
    kaddish for, II, 132; CCAR, II, 138
    priest (Kohne) I, 196
    reverting, I, 195; II, 120
    shiva for, III, 181
    status of, II, 120; CCAR, II, 127
    wedding attendants, VII, 189
Ark:
    backs to the, VII, 15
    bowing before, IV, 78
    curtain, I, 62
    dance troupe before, IV, 179
    disused, VII, 24
    embroidered name of God on curtain, III, 22
    location of, I, 65
    open during service, I, 43; V, 37
    standing while open, V, 38
    used as a bookcase, VII, 26
    wedding before the, VII, 182
Artificial insemination: I, 212, 217
Ashes:
    buried at home, V, 169

    burial of cremation ashes, VI, 112
    mother's ashes in son's grave, III, 145
    of cremation in Temple cornerstone, VI, 167
Ashkenazim:
    age at Bar Mitzvah, III, 70
    Chanukah lights, I, 25
Athletics and sports: III, 231
    in community center on Sabbath, IV, 11
Autopsy:
    as funeral heading, I, 130
    increased polemics, V, 216

Baptism:
    by Jewish nurse, II, 67
    of child before adoption, II, 97
Bareheadedness:
    see Toupee, IV, 302
Bar Mitzvah:
    an announcement, VI, 18
    and quarrelling family, V, 27
    at age of twelve, III, 70
    caterer and Sabbath, III, 225
    divorced father, I, 33
    error in reciting Torah blessing, IV, 56
    Gentile stepfather, III, 91
    Havdala, VI, 33
    Havdala early, VI, 37
    in legal literature, V, 27
    Mincha, VI, 35
    of uncircumcised boy, III, 107
    on Friday night, II, 22
    on Yizkor days, VI, 16
    party, VI, 38
    retarded child, II, 23
    Sabbath afternoon, I, 37; II, 19
    stepfather called up, I, 32
    Sunday, I, 35
    Yom Kippur, I, 38

Bas Mitzvah: II, 19; VI, 20
    duty of father to train daughter, VI,
        21
    Obadiah Joseph, VI, 24
Bastardy: I, 201, 203
    Karaites, III, 186
Bereaved:
    comforting them on the Sabbath, VII,
        130
    visiting them, VII, 133
Birth control: I, 206
Blind:
    duties of, III, 74
    with seeing eye dog at services, III,
        74
Blood from the dead: III, 242
    transfusion, III, 121
Body:
    bequeathing parts of, V, 216
    infectious, refusing to handle, V, 181
    freezing, for later funeral, VII, 100
    lost at sea, I, 147
    lost but found later, VII, 142
    ownership of the, VII, 79
    position of in grave, V, 172
    preparing on Sabbath, I, 126
    quicklime on the, VII, 117
    remains to science, I, 130; IV, 278
    surgical transplants, III, 118
    which to bury first, V, 165
Bowing:
    before Ark, IV, 78
    on Yom Kippur, III, 49; IV, 79
Brain:
    injury of, IV, 192
Breaking glass at weddings: II, 182
    Jacob Z. Lauterbach, II, 183
    Hillel Posek, II, 186
    see, also, Wedding
Breast feeding: II, 226
    kinship affected by, IV, 308
Bride:
    bridesmaids, I, 190
    not seen by groom, I, 182
    pregnant, V, 64
Bride and groom:
    under talit, IV, 294
Bridegroom:

impotent, IV, 121
    not seeing bride, I, 182
    soldier wearing sword, IV, 116
Bride's veil: III, 188
Building fund, rebates from a, VII, 168
Burial:
    arrangement of graves, I, 156
    Christian cemetery, I, 140
    Christian funeral, rabbi participating,
        III, 175
    crypts, IV, 254
    delayed, I, 150; V, 163
    enemies side by side, I, 136; II, 61
    family crypts, IV, 254
    funeral and burial at night, VI, 158
    in his or her city, V, 185
    in Israel, without talit, IV, 271
    in national cemetery, VII, 105
    infant in grave of parent, II, 139
    Jewish, of a convert, V, 240
    mass burials, III, 169
    men and women side by side, IV, 260
    mother's ashes in son's grave, III,
        145
    non-Jews in Jewish cemetery, III, 155
    of an apostate, II, 127
    of cremation ashes, VI, 112
    of cremation ashes at home, V, 169
    of fallen Israeli soldiers, V, 205
    of infant, I, 96
    of pet animals, III, 165
    of second wife, VI, 172
    of still-born, V, 158
    of suicides, V, 254
    on festivals, I, 49
    on holidays after a strike, V, 163
    sequence of, after a strike, V, 165
    sinner, II, 131
    some duties, V, 189
    son's presence barred from, VI, 282
    three day delay, IV, 189
    tombstone in absence of body, III,
        141
    without family or kaddish, IV, 274
    see, also, Cemetery

Caesarean operation:
    Maimonides discusses, I, 216

on a dead woman, I, 213; V, 212
on a dying woman, I, 212
Candle lighting:
and Kiddush, dispute over, VII, 26
at Kol Nidre, V, 60
Candles:
at Saturday night Seder, VI, 40
composition and size of Sabbath candles, V, 49
in home on Yom Kippur, custom, V, 62
Sabbath lights on table, IV, 91
Cannibalism: VI, 271
Cantor:
questions from Social Security, III, 213
reciting *tefilah* with, IV, 18
serving as rabbi, III, 211
Casket: covering the, VII, 152
Cemetery:
a former Christian c., VII, 85
alignment of graves, III, 132
Arlington, I, 141
burial of Jew in Christian c., I, 140
burial of non-Jew in Jewish c., III, 154; VII, 85
disinterment of Jew for reburial, III, 162
disinterment of Jew for reburial in Christian c., VI, 179
eternal flame, IV, 249
first grave, III, 138
municipal and Jewish sections, I, 161
objection to perpetual light in, VI, 106
of defunct congregation, IV, 240
outright possession preferable, II, 148
section in general c., II, 144
Sefer Torah carried into, II, 43
selling part of, VI, 128
synagogue near, II, 41
vandalized, V, 224
visiting before thirty days, VI, 109, 100
visiting on Sabbath and holidays, VI, 188
visiting the, V, 232
work on Rosh Hashonah, VII, 37

see also Burial, Tombstone
Cemetery memorial service:
on second day Rosh Hashonah, VI, 57
Central Conference of American Rabbis (CCAR):
I, 87 Mixed Marriage and Intermarriage
II, 120 Suicides
II, 127 Status of Apostates
II, 138 Kaddish for Apostates and Gentiles
II, 188 Abortion
III, 62 Unworthy Man called to Torah
III, 84 Expulsion of Member from the Congregation
III, 103 Anesthetic for Circumcision
III, 112 Ethiopian "Hebrew" Congregation
III, 118 Surgical Transplants
III, 141 Tombstone in Absence of Body
III, 154 Burial of Non-Jews in Jewish Cemetery
III, 186 Marriage with Karaites
III, 199 Rabbinical Fees and Salaries
Chanukah: I, 29
children lighting Chanukah lights, I, 26
lights, I, 25; IV, 90
memorial service, I, 29
men's obligation to light candles, I, 25
non-linear arrangement of lights, IV, 87
shamash ("servant") IV, 90
Chapel named for individual: VII, 9
Chaplain's insignia:
Hebrew letters on, V, 120
Charity:
status of recipients, VI, 65
Charoses: VII, 265
Chaverus:
Ethical Culturists, III, 183
Jews raised as Christians, III, 217
promise of, II, 123
Chevra Kadisha: I, 128
not using the, VII, 114

Child named:
  after deceased person, IV, 136
  after Gentile grandparents, IV, 134
Children:
  adoption of, of mixed race, III, 196
  Christian service, attendance at, I, 115
  Christian Sunday school, II, 59
  Christmas celebration at school, I, 112
  custody of, I, 33, 200, 209; III, 193
  lighting Chanukah candles, I, 26
Children ("Sons") of Noah: I, 89, 110, 114, 116; IV, 71
Christian cemetery:
  a former, VII, 85
  body of Jew to, III, 163; VI, 179
  burial of Jew in, I, 140
  convert buried in, V, 151
  disinterment from, VI, 175
  memorial service in, I, 143
  officiating for Christians, III, 175
  worshiping in, I, 144
Christians:
  not idolators, IV, 71
  officiating at funerals of, III, 175
  relatives memorialized, IV, 226
  Sefer Torah, called to, III, 49
  "Sons of Noah," IV, 71
  substituting for on Christmas, V, 131
  taught Torah, V, 47
  temple organ used for Christian hymns, II, 47
Christmas:
  celebration of in school, I, 112
Chuppah: III, 190
Church:
  use of synagogue building, V, 44
Church membership and conversion: I, 82
Circumcision:
  anesthetic for, III, 103; CCAR, III, 103
  Bar Mitzvah for uncircumcised, III, 107
  before eighth day, I, 90
  CCAR debate, VI, 71
  child of unmarried mother, III, 100

child of unmarried couple, VII, 58
children of mixed marriage, IV, 165
Christian surgeon, I, 93, 111
dead child, I, 96
"Ethiopian Hebrew" congregations, III, 112
Gentile doctor, VI, 93
irreligious Jewish doctor, VI, 92
Jewish adult, I, 100
naming of orphan, II, 91
naming when circumcision is delayed, II, 94
of proselytes, VI, 71
on eighth day, I, 38
on Yom Kippur, I, 38
son of Gentile wife, II, 99
who may circumcise, I, 105
woman doctor, VI, 90
Coffin: I, 155
  covering the, VII, 152
  keys in the, VII, 262
  lights at head of, V, 177
  plain blanket used to conceal, VII, 42
  re-use of, I, 135
  two in one grave, VI, 100
  wife's ashes in husband's coffin, IV, 237
  wooden nails for, II, 153
Committal services omitted: VI, 148
Community Centers:
  and Sabbath, VI, 11
  sports, VI, 11
  swimming pool open, VI, 13
Competing Gentile Undertaker: VII, 164
Competition unfair: IV, 281
Confession:
  for the dying, I, 124
  knowledge of a crime, III, 205
Congregation:
  absentee vote, VI, 224
  English name for, I, 78
  expulsion from, III, 84
  gift corner, I, 51
  homosexual, I, 23
  majority or unanimous rule, VI, 226
  meeting on the Sabbath, I, 46
  membership of mixed couple, II, 63

Seder, I, 55
social hall, I, 75
Succah, I, 60
using cemetery money, VII, 109
Contributors:
changing purpose of gift, IV, 138, 229
criminal contributors, III, 52
listing names of, II, 203
rabbis to building fund, II, 215
to synagogue from criminals, III, 52
Conversion:
a married woman, I, 85
and church membership, I, 82
answers to Israel on, V, 269
CCAR, I, 87, mixed marriage and intermarriage
conducted by layman, III, 96
dubious, V, 136
incomplete, IV, 154; VII, 75
insincerity of, IV, 157
indelible allegiance, II, 126
infants, III, 80
man, when family remains Christian, III, 215
marriage of a Gentile wife, II, 5
marriage with Ethical Culturists, III, 183
of Negroes, II, 83
preconverts and Sabbath lights, III, 88
questionable, II, 78
reconverting ex-nun, V, 141
Reform attitude to, IV, 157
reverting proselyte, IV, 159
unprovable claim to, II, 87; III, 219
without marriage, I, 87
woman, when children remain Christian, III, 110
see also, Miscegenation, II, 83
Convert:
and Jewish burial, V, 240
and rabbi's responsibility, VI, 66
buried in Christian cemetery, V, 151
surname of, IV, 148
Copyrighting:
of books, V, 245
Cornea of the dead used: VI, 153
Cremation: IV, 148

ashes buried at home, V, 169
ashes in temple cornerstone, VI, 167
bodies donated to science, IV, 278
family disagreement over, V, 228
mother's ashes in son's grave, III, 145
wife's ashes in husband's coffin, IV, 237
Cryobiology: III, 238
see "Freezing of Bodies"
Crypts as family burial places: IV, 254
Curtain, Ark: I, 62

Dance:
on Sabbath, II, 32
troupe before Ark, IV, 179
Dead:
blood, using of, III, 242
clothes and shoes of the, I, 175; II, 149
cornea of, VI, 153
ownership of the body of the, VII, 79
pardon asked of the, V, 293
photographing the, VI, 169
removed on Sabbath, VI, 163
shoes for the, II, 149
talit for, IV, 269
wishes of, I, 137
Death:
body lost at sea, I, 147
child before Bar Mitzvah, I, 167
dates of, II, 148
determination of, IV, 188
donating body, I, 130; IV, 278
euthanasia, I, 118
hastening of, I, 118, 215; IV, 201
Kaddish for unmarried child, I, 167
last hours, IV, 195
postponement of, IV, 188
presumption of, II, 107
Sabbath, preparing body, I, 126
surgical transplants, III, 118
terminal patient, IV, 197
time of despair, II, 105
Deconsecration:
of old synagogue, V, 9
of synagogue in large city, V, 10
Dedication of a synagogue: V, 9

Deprogramming Young People: VII, 231
Disinterment:
    due to labor strike, V, 160
    from Christian cemetery, VI, 175
    of Jew from Jewish cemetery for reburial in Christian cemetery, VI, 179
    services at reburial, VI, 177
Distribution of Laws in Jewish Legal Literature: VII, 267
Divorce:
    father, natural and Bar Mitzvah, I, 33
    father, obligation, I, 33
    for doubtful marriage, V, 82
    daughter, custody of, III, 193
Dog:
    burial of, III, 165
    seeing-eye dog at services, III, 74
Drugs, psychedelic: III, 247
Duchan: I, 41
Dues:
    synagogue, nonpayment of, IV, 179
Dying patient:
    Caesarean operation for dying woman, I, 212
    in agony, asks for death, VI, 85
    infant, naming of, IV, 223
    informed of condition, I, 122
    kept alive, I, 117; terminal, IV, 197
    last hours chaye sha'a, VI, 88
    organ transplants, III, 118
    relieving pain of, VI, 84
    requests no funeral, II, 110

Earthquakes: V, 290
Electronic eavesdropping:
    and Jewish law, VI, 260
    privacy of private premises, VI, 265
    prohibition against self-incrimination, VI, 265
English name for congregation: I, 78
Erusin: I, 182
Esther and second Seder: VI, 303
Eternal flame: III, 8
    in cemetery, IV, 249
    on grave, VI, 106
"Ethiopian Hebrews": III, 112

Etrog:
    frozen, III, 26
    last year's, III, 48
Eulogy: I, 27
    for a Christian, I, 145; III, 175
    for a suicide, II, 119
    post-funeral, VII, 119
Eunich (saris): I, 27
Euthanasia: I, 118
Excommunication, laws of: IV, 180

Falashas as Jews: V, 297
Falasha woman: II, 85
Fallen Israeli soldiers:
    temporary burial of, V, 205
Fast:
    proclaiming a new, VI, 47
Fast Days:
    marriage on, II, 4
Fasting:
    if Torah dropped, V, 117
Father's name forgotten: V, 32
Feebleminded:
    and Bar Mitzvah, II, 23
    sterilizing the, V, 74
Fertility pill: VI, 205
Fertilized ovum implant: VI, 215
Festival:
    burial on, I, 49
Flowers:
    belated, VI, 108
    planted on grave, V, 284
Foetal material:
    study of, V, 155; V, 256
Food:
    diminishing world supply, VI, 63
Foundling:
    "son of Abraham," V, 34
Freezing of bodies (cryobiology): III, 238
Funeral:
    and burial at night, VI, 158
    Christian, rabbi participating, III, 175
    congregational charge for, V, 193
    double, II, 138
    eulogy after, VII, 119
    for those lost at sea, II, 104
    freezing a body for later funeral, VII, 100

from temple, VI, 95
Gentile funerals on Sabbath, VI, 142
halted at synagogue, VI, 182
mass burial, III, 169
omission of committal service, VI,
    148
requests no funeral, II, 110
services for ex-members, V, 200
services for non-members, V, 196
services in synagogue without body,
    I, 27: IV, 274
visiting another grave after, VI, 187
washing hands after, VI, 293
Funeral folklore: I, 174; II, 148; VII, 262

Gambling:
    for synagogue, III, 56
    occasional, VI, 229
    state legalized lotteries, VI, 231
Garnishee of wages: V, 260
Gentile:
    bridesmaids, I, 190
    buried in Jewish cemetery, VII, 88
    burial of non-Jews in Jewish ceme-
        tery, III, 154
    CCAR, II, 138, Kaddish for
    funerals on the Sabbath, VI, 142
    Kaddish for, II, 132
    marrying, I, 186
    membership in synagogue, VI, 221
    musicians, I, 191
    obstetrician, I, 111
    officiating at funeral of, III, 175
    officiating at marriage of, I, 186
    participating in Sabbath service, VII,
        33
    president for sisterhood, VI, 249
    stepfather at Bar Mitzvah, III, 91
    talit and mezuzahs to Gentiles, VI, 25
    visitors and Kaddish, IV, 62
German measles: II, 188
Get:
    and Reform Rabbis, III, 218
    modern, V, 3
God's Name:
    destroying, III, 29
    embroidered on ark curtain, III, 22
    icing on cakes, III, 20

painted on wall, III, 30
printed on stationery, III, 224
spelled "G-d," II, 50
Grafting:
    fruit, VI, 284
    roses, II, 222
Grandson and grandfather:
    mutual duties between, V, 281
Grave:
    alignment of, III, 132
    ashes buried at home, V, 169
    depth of, IV, 230
    mother's ashes in son's grave, III,
        145
    of Oriental Jews covered with flat
        stone, II, 142
    perpetual light on, VI, 104
    plantings or flowers on, V, 284
    position of body in, V, 172
    two coffins in one, VI, 100
    unfilled, VII, 97
    vacated, re-use of, I, 132
    visiting another, I, 176; VI, 187

Halacha:
    and Reform Judaism, I, Introduction,
        p.3
    and space travel, VII, 243
    in Orthodoxy, I, Introduction, pp. 4
        ff.
Halloween masks, etc.: III, 93
Hatred, avoiding: II, 72
Hearse, rented: VI, 122
Hebrew:
    date for tombstone, I, 169
    date of yahrzeit, I, 169
    letters on Chaplain's insignia, V, 120
High-rise church and residence: VI, 306
Homosexual congregation: V, 23
Homosexuality: III, 236
Hospice, the: VII, 67
Hypnotism: VII, 250
Hysterectomy: VI, 211

Identity:
    who is a Jew, II, 73
Individual:
    naming the sanctuary after an. VII, 7

Infant:
  conversion of, III, 80
  circumcision of a dead infant, I, 96
  dying, status of, IV, 223
Insemination with mixed seed, VII, 202
Israel:
  Jewish religion in, II, 76
  questions on proselytism from, V, 269
  visit to, V, 69

Jewish nurse, dying Catholic infant: II, 67
Joint *mikveh* and baptistry: VI, 274

Kaddish:
  adopted son, I, 26
  after study, II, 18
  apostate, Gentiles, II, 132
  as legal duty, I, 166
  CCAR Yearbook 1957, II, 138, for apostates
  congregational, II, 27
  customs, III, 179
  for a child, I, 165
  for first wife, I, 162
  for Gentile, II, 136
  for Gentile parents, IV, 63
  three steps backward, II, 217
  with Gentile visitors, IV, 62
  various types, I, 32
  worshiping alone, II, 14
"Keriah" ribbon: VI, 279
Kiddush:
  dispute over candle-lighting and, VII, 28
  in the synagogue, VII, 29
  standing or sitting during the, VII, 29
  wine at congregational, II, 27
Kidney transplants: VII, 62
Kohen:
  adoption by, V, 145
  extra shrouds for, V, 276
  marrying daughter of a mixed marriage, II, 158
Kol Nidre:
  candle-lighting at, V, 60
  United Jewish Appeal at, V, 57

Law:
  civil, I, 7
  guidance not governance, I, 22
  Reform and Halacha, III, 4
Lights:
  at head of coffin, V, 177
  Chanukah, I, 24; IV, 90
  children lighting Chanukah lights, I, 26
  eternal *(ner tamid)* III, 8
  memorial, at home, III, 129
  men lighting Chanukah candles, I, 25
  men lighting Sabbath candles, I, 25
  perpetual, on grave, VI, 104
  pre-convert and Sabbath lights, III, 88
  Sabbath, I, 24; on table, IV, 91
  unmarried woman and Sabbath lights, I, 24
Loaves:
  Sabbath, pre-sliced, IV, 95
Lulav and Esrog after Succos: VII, 48

Malpractice suits and the physician: VII, 224
Mamzer: IV, 104
  adoption, I, 200
  naming child of unmarried mother, V, 91
Marital rights of a raped woman: VI, 216
  Jewish law on side of victim, VI, 220
Marranos: I, 80, 86, 195; II, 121
  converted to Judaism, II, 121
  woman raised as Christian, III, 217
Marriage:
  apostate daughter, I, 192
  barren wife, II, 155
  bride's veil, III, 188
  CCAR, I, 87, mixed marriage and intermarriage
  civil, validity of, VII, 195
  civil, mixed, II, 65
  doubtful, divorce for, V, 82
  erusin, I, 182
  Ethical Culturists, III, 183
  Karaites, III, 186
  Levirate, III, 221

marrying a trans-sexual, VI, 196
mixed marriage on Temple premises, IV, 108
of a Gentile wife, II, 5
on fast days, II, 4
pregnant girl, IV, 103
raped woman, VI, 216
Reform formula, VI, 191
Reform marriage and Orthodox aspersions, II, 194
remarriage to first husband, II, 163
two Gentiles, I, 186
with half-aunt, IV, 100
without *chalitza,* III, 221
without license, V, 98
without rabbi or Hebrew, VI, 200
woman raised as Christian, III, 217
Marrying the sterlized: V, 78
Mausoleums:
communal, I, 158
private, I, 159
Membership:
CCAR expulsion, III, 84
expulsion, III, 84
Gentile membership in synagogue, VI, 221
mixed couples, II, 63
unmarried couples and temple membership, VI, 238
Memorial:
candles for Yom Kippur, III, 14
changing name on memorial windows, IV, 138
Christian relatives, IV, 226
lights in the home, III, 129
lists on Sabbath, III, 178; IV, 24
lists, titles in, VII, 41
lists, whether to shorten, IV, 24
Memorial service:
for lost body, I, 147
in cemetery, second day Rosh Hashonah, VI, 57
in Christian cemetery, I, 143
on Sabbath, I, 26
Menopause: II, 219
Menorah:
and the Two Tablets, IV, 37
as floor decoration, I, 68

made from Torah ornaments, III, 19
made from metal Torah rollers, III, 37
non-linear Chanukah menorah, IV, 86
Mezuzah:
affixed diagonally, VI, 82
glass, VII, 53
printed, VII, 17
to Gentiles, VI, 27
Midwifery: I, 188
Mikveh:
joint with baptistry, VI, 274
Mirrors, covering of: I, 179
Miscegenation: II, 83
Mixed couple:
temple membership, II, 63
Mixed marriage:
CCAR attitude to, IV, 112
circumcision of children of, IV, 165
Kohen and child of, II, 158
on temple premises, IV, 108
Mohel:
woman doctor, VI, 90
Money matters on Sabbath: I, 47
Mother's name:
in Yizkor, VI, 120
on son's tombstone, VI, 116
when praying for sick, VI, 120
Mourning:
covering mirrors, I, 179
dates of, in different time zones, IV, 243
delayed burial, I, 151
dishes returned, I, 178
dying request, no mourning, II, 110
cremated, VII, 139
for dead soldiers, V, 210
for stillborn and infants, I, 166
for suicides, II, 119; II, 129
greeting mourners, III, 156
greeting, visiting mourners, III, 125
when body lost, I, 147, 150; II, 104
Muggers:
on Sabbath, VI, 28
Museum case, Torah in: V, 110
Music in synagogue:
organ and Christian, II, 47
secular music, III, 33

Name:
  changed for convert, IV, 148
  father's, forgotten, V, 32
Naming:
  child of unmarried mother, V, 91
  delayed circumcision, II, 94
  name changed for convert, IV, 148
  of child after Gentile grandparent, IV, 134
  of congregation, I, 78
  of dying infant, IV, 223
  of orphan, II, 91
  the sanctuary after an individual, VII, 7
Negroes:
  see Races
New Testament:
  rabbi reading, IV, 73
New Year:
  shofar on Sabbath, II, 36
Night clubs rented for High Holiday services: VII, 13

Oath of office: V, 279
Operetta in the sanctuary: VII, 11
Ordination, annulling rabbi's: VI, 232
Orthodoxy and the Halacha: I, Introduction, pp. 4 ff.

Pants suit, lady's: V, 123
Pardon asked of the dead: V, 293
Parent, aged, to nursing home, VII, 92
Passover:
  eighth day on Sabbath, III, 42
  spices prohibited, V, 287
Patient:
  dying, kept alive, I, 117
  informed of condition, I, 122
  relieving pain of dying patient, VI, 84
  terminal, allowed to die, IV, 197
  which to save, IV, 203
Penitential prayers: I, 27
Physician:
  atheistic, I, 109
  Christian, I, 93
  circumcising, I, 106
  divine emissary, I, 119
  Jewish, I, 107

Pidyen ha-Ben: V, 28
  possible pidyen of second son, VI, 266
  one child by Caesarean, VI, 267
Plants or flowers on grave: V, 284
Pornography: III, 240
Posul Torah in Ark: V, 114
Prayerbooks, burning of: I, 71
Priest (Kohen)
  apostate, I, 196
  community composed of, I, 40, 41
  marrying daughter of mixed marriage, II, 158
Printed Mezuzahs, VII, 17
Prohibitions, Biblical and Reform: IV, 102
Proselyte:
  accepted into family, IV, 162
  born anew, I, 84
  circumcision of, VI, 71
  indelible allegiance of, IV, 162
  Jewish name for, VII, 72
  methods of reception, II, 74, 79
  pregnant, IV, 143
  questions concerning, VII, 72
  reverting, IV, 159
Proselytism:
  questions from Israel on, V, 269
Prostration: I, 70
  before Ark, IV, 78
  on Yom Kippur, III, 49
Protest, halting religious services as a: IV, 82

Rabbi:
  annulling ordination, VI, 232
  contributing to building fund, II, 215
  officiating with Karaites, III, 186
  participating in Christian funeral, III, 175
  reading or responding to passages in New Testament, IV, 73
Rabbinate:
  fees and salary, III, 199
  questions from Social Security, III, 209
Rabbinical tenure: V, 263

Race:
adopting mulatto children, III, 196
"Ethiopian" congregations, III, 112
mixture of, I, 200; II, 85
Raped woman, marital rights: VI, 216
Rebates from a building fund, VII, 168
Reconversion of ex-nun: V, 141
Red Cross, identification card of: IV, 175
Redemption *(pidyen ha-ben):* V, 29
father's right absolute, V, 30
Reform:
and *mamzerus,* VII, 256
and spiritualism, VII, 252
attitude to conversion, IV, 157
Reform Judaism:
and the Halachic tradition, I, 3
attitude to law, II, 8
change, VI, 4
marriage formula, VI, 191
Remarriage:
of Russian immigrants, VII, 193
of a widower, VII, 198
Responsa:
computerizing, VI, 2
first Reform literature, VI, 5
statistical survey, VI, 3
Rosh Hashonah:
mood of, VI, 58
shofar on New Year Sabbath, II, 36
two days in Israel, IV, 286

Sabbath:
caterer working in synagogue on, III, 225
comforting the bereaved on the, VII, 130
communal business planned on, V, 58
congregational meetings on, I, 46
eighth day Passover, III, 42
Gentile funerals on, VI, 142
Gift Corner open, I, 51
healing sick, VI, 30
hiring musicians, II, 35
lights, I, 24; on table, IV, 91
loaves, pre-sliced, IV, 95
memorial mood, VI, 59
memorial service, I, 26

men lighting Sabbath candles, I, 25
muggers and money, VI, 28
money matters on Sabbath, I, 47
moving bodies of dead soldiers on, V, 210
muktsa, VI, 29
New Year shofar, II, 36
preparing body, I, 126
reading memorial list on, IV, 24
removing dead on, VI, 163
service, Gentile's part in, VII, 33
school dance on, II, 32
sports in community center, VI, 11
unmarried woman and Sabbath lights, I, 24
wedding on, II, 167
Sabbath candles:
composition and size of, V, 49
prekindled in synagogue, VI, 9
Sabbath candlesticks:
weekday use of, V, 53
Sacred objects:
menorah and two tablets, IV, 37
ranking of, I, 62; II, 48
selling, III, 19
Torah decorations, VI, 31
Torah rollers, III, 36
Salt for the bread blessing: VII, 247
Samaritans: I, 64
Sanctuary:
an operetta in the, VII, 11
named after an individual, VII, 7
School prayerbook:
assembling a, VII, 219
Seder:
candles at Saturday night Seder, VI, 40
congregational, I, 55
Esther and second Seder, VI, 303
wine, types of, III, 43
Sefer Torah: See Torah
Services:
Ark open, V, 37
dog, seeing-eye at, III, 74
interfaith, IV, 69
halting, as a protest, IV, 82
lengthened on Yom Kippur, V, 59
memorial on Sabbath, I, 26

places to conduct, I, 76
pre-converts participating in, III, 88
Sha'atnez with regard to *tzitzis:* VI, 296
Shiva:
  and quarreling family, VI, 136
  for converted son, III, 182
  in house where deceased died, VI, 138
  in Jerusalem, VII, 125
  lights, III, 129
  on half-holidays, III, 225
Shofar:
  New Year Sabbath, II, 36
Shroud, extra, for Kohen: V, 276
Sinai, stones from, for Decalogue tablets: IV, 40
Social hall of synagogue: I, 75
Social Security:
  wedding without a license, V, 98
Soldier:
  Israeli, entering synagogue with rifle, IV, 119
  wearing sword at wedding, IV, 117
Space travel: VII, 243
Spices:
  which prohibited for Passover use, V, 287
Sports:
  and athletics, III, 231
  on Sabbath in community center, VI, 11
Stained-glass window named for individual: VII, 9
Statuettes in synagogue: V, 127
Status Quo group, Hungary: I, 82
Stepfather at Bar Mitzvah: I, 32
Sterilization of feebleminded: V, 74
Sterilized:
  marrying of, V, 78
Sterilizing husband: I, 206
Succah:
  and artificial fruit, VII, 46
  congregational, I, 60
  permanent, VI, 44
Suicides: II, 114
  burial of, V, 254
  CCAR Yearbook, 1959, II, 120
  Dr. Jacob Z. Lauterbach, II, 114

eulogy, II, 119
failed, II, 117
great stress, II, 117
noble martyrdom, II, 116
to dissuade, V, 253
Surgery, cosmetic: VI, 287
Surgical transplants:
  CCAR, III, 118
  pig's heart valve, IV, 217
  trans-sexuals, IV, 128
Survivor's sense of guilt: VII, 179
Sustenance, order of: VI, 63
Synagogue:
  Bagdad, I, 61
  building used by church, V, 44
  candles, prekindled, VI, 9
  collecting pledges through civil courts, II, 206
  converted from funeral parlor, VI, 145
  dedication of, V, 9
  gambling for, III, 56
  Gentile membership, VI, 221
  gifts from criminal, III, 52
  gift to, IV, 140
  halting funeral at, VI, 182
  in joint building with Unitarian Church, V, 18
  in large city, deconsecrated, V, 10
  Menorah decoration in floor, I, 68
  near cemetery, II, 41
  old, deconsecrated, V, 9
  orientation, I, 66
  permanent ownership of, V, 20
  portrait bust in, IV, 184
  rabbis contributing to building fund, II, 215
  regulations, two questions on, IV, 179
  sale of to Black Muslims, V, 13
  sanctity of unfinished building, II, 210
  secular music in, III, 33
  social hall of, I, 75
  statues in, V, 127
  unfinished building, II, 210

Table, Sabbath lights on: IV, 91

Talit:
  and *mezuzah* to Gentiles, VI, 25
  at Torah reading, VII, 20
  bride and groom under, IV, 294
  for the dead, IV, 269
  in Reform service, IV, 46
  not to be worn at night, VII, 21
  women wearing, IV, 52
Tefilah, reciting with a cantor: IV, 18
Tefillin:
  laying of at Bar Mitzvah, III, 70
  when Torah dropped, V, 117
  while carrying Torah, III, 38
Temple membership:
  and charity, VII, 175
  of unmarried couple, VI, 238
  pilegesh, VI, 241
Testifying against a fellow Jew: VI, 252
  dina d'malchuso, VI, 253
  Isserles on forgers, VI, 255
Test-tube baby, the: VII, 205
Tetragrammaton: III, 22; III, 224
Titles in memorial list: VII, 41
Tobacco:
  care of health, Torah warning, VI, 56
  harm to self, VI, 55
  smoking, blessing before, VI, 51
  the use of, VI, 50
Tombstone:
  anywhere in cemetery, II, 109
  at the head, II, 143
  behalf of living, II, 109
  CCAR, III, 141
  exchanging of a, V, 236
  Hebrew, I, 169
  in absence of body, III, 141
  is a t. mandatory, VII, 147
  location of, II, 141
  mother's name on son's, VI, 116
  name missing on, II, 107
  pebble on, VI, 291
  photograph on, VI, 118
  removing of, III, 149
  secular date on, I, 168; VI, 118
  special committees in Europe to
    watch over, VI, 107
  uniformity of, I, 154
Torah:

ark closed, I, 435
auctioning of, III, 60
blessings, errors in reciting, IV, 56
blind people called to, III, 75
calling people to, without name and
  Hebrew patronymic, V, 33
carried, how, III, 38
carried into cemetery, II, 43
CCAR, unworthy man called to, III,
  62
Catholic priest, reading from, IV, 76
Christians, II, 49
covers, white, III, 25
covers, worn-out, VII, 24
decorations, III, 18; IV, 31
eighth day of Passover, III, 42
fasting if dropped, V, 117
in jails and asylums, III, 77
in museum case or ark, V, 110
in procession, IV, 14
on Friday, IV, 14
ornaments of, IV, 31
ownership of, V, 104
posul, in ark, V, 114
preserving a fragment of, VI, 80
reading, *tallis* at, VII, 20
reading translated verse by verse, V,
  40
rollers, III, 36
sold to support rabbi, VI, 245
taught to non-Jews, V, 47
two brothers called to, VI, 278
unworthy man called up for, III, 62
white mantles, III, 25
woman called up for, I, 40
Toupee:
  bareheadedness, IV, 302
Transplant:
  of kidney, VII, 62
  of pig's heart valves, IV, 217
Transplanted ovum: VII, 213
Trans-sexuals, surgery for: IV, 128
  performing marriage for, VI, 196
Two brothers called to Torah: VI, 278

Undertaker, the competing Gentile:
  VII, 164
Undertaking business, the: VII, 158

Unitarian Church:
  in joint building with synagogue, V,
    18
  Jewish member of, II, 56
United Jewish Appeal at Kol Nidre: V,
  57
U'n'sana Tokef: VI, 300
"Unwanted" child, the: VII, 239

Visiting the bereaved, VII, 133

Wages garnisheed: V, 260
Wedding:
  before open ark, VII, 182
  borrowed ring, II, 178
  breaking glass, II, 182-3, 186
  Gentile bridesmaids, I, 190
  groom not seeing bride, I, 182
  in Temple, I, 198
  Moses Isserles and Sabbath, II, 169
  on Hoshana Rabba, II, 170
  on Ninth of Av, II, 173
  Saturday before dark, II, 167
  soldier wearing sword at, IV, 116
  sound-taping of, II, 53
  trans-sexuals, VI, 196
  without license, V, 98
  see also, Marriage
Who is a Jew: II, 73
Wine:
  congregational Kiddush, II, 27

types of, at Seder, III, 43
Woman:
  barren, II, 155
  doctor, as *mohel,* VI, 90
  married convert, I, 85
  returned to first husband, II, 163
  unmarried and Sabbath lights, I, 24
  wearing pants suit, V, 123
  wearing *talit,* IV, 52
  wearing wig, III, 227
Women called to Torah: I, 40

Yahrzeit:
  for a child, I, 165
  kaddish when worshiping alone, II,
    14
  observance of, IV, 30
  secular date for, I, 168; II, 17
Yizkor: I, 164
  during first year, I, 177
  prayer developed on three festivals,
    IV, 25
Yom Kippur:
  Bar Mitzvah, I, 36
  bowing and kneeling on, IV, 79
  circumcision, I, 38
  memorial candles on, III, 14

Zodiac, signs of, on synagogue windows: VII, 56